Serving
with
Power

SERVING WITH POWER

Reviving the Spirit of Christian Ministry

Kortright Davis

PAULIST PRESS
New York/Mahwah, N.J.

Cover design by Cindy Dunne

Library of Congress Cataloging-in-Publication Data

Davis, Kortright.
Serving with power : reviving the spirit of Christian ministry / by Kortright Davis.
p. cm.
Includes bibliographical references.
ISBN 0-8091-3890-5 (alk. paper)
1. Clergy—Office. 2. Pastoral theology. I. Title.
BV660.2.D38   1999
253—dc21   99-32696
                                                    CIP

Published by Paulist Press
997 Macarthur Boulevard
Mahwah, New Jersey 07430

www.paulistpress.com

Printed and bound in the
United States of America

Contents

INTRODUCTION

THERE OFTEN COMES A TIME IN THE LIFE OF THE CHURCH when codes and customs, values and virtues, even words and symbols, become worn and jaded. They seem to lose much of their force and efficacy and no longer command any authority in people's lives. Passages of scripture become too familiar to be challenging. Sermons become too boring to be arresting. Moments of prayer and patterns of piety become void of their deepest meaning. Is this all a result of the nature of religion itself? Does religion eventually lose its hold on its adherents because of the repetitive way in which it has to be carried out? Or does it become ineffective because it simply loses its mystique, its sense of mystery, or its authority? Does Christian spirituality itself become hostage to the forces of boredom?

Much of our religious and theological activity is heavily dependent upon the power of words. We place high value and almost supernatural significance on the meaning of some words over others. Some have evocative appeal. Some create feelings of awe and reverence. Some point beyond themselves to spheres of meaning and aspiration that are not attainable in any other way. Yet words also lose their power, at least for the time being. Nevertheless, we cannot do without them. They serve the unique purpose of not only expressing who we are and what we mean by what we feel or fear, but they also connect us with the whole world of meaning and enlightenment around us. Words not only have power, they also have authority. Such is the nature of laws, rules, and mandates through which we seek to organize and control our affairs.

What does the word *ministry* really mean? Why has it become so popular, and yet so vague, within the current culture of our churches? It often seems to generate a wide variety of meanings and uses, depending on who uses it, or who hears it. Our ecclesial traditions have not always been clear about whether we really mean "service," or whether we mean "authority," or "power," or even "duty." When Jesus of Nazareth uses the term in the gospel story, he clearly renounces any sense of power or authority, and gives himself unconditionally to that self-sacrificing life of service and obedience to the God whom he calls "Father." In so doing, he speaks of himself as one who is among others as a servant, a minister. In that self-understanding, the power of God to heal, transform, and liberate is made available to all who accept Jesus. His is a life of *serving with power.* This provides for us the main optic through which we can discern not only the meaning of the word *ministry* itself, but also the power of service which evolves from the witness of all those who follow Jesus as the Word of God made flesh through serving.

This book is an attempt to explore the power of the Word of God in shaping the contours of Christian ministry, in shaping the mandate for sharing the gospel, the good news of faith, with others, and in creating new possibilities for practicing the power of the word, in the fellowship of the Spirit. It is God's word that both sets us free and unites. It is God's word that both calls us together and sends us forth for more powerful service. It is God's word that both creates a world and recreates it. It is God's word that both destroys that which ought not to be, and generates that which ought to exist. But where is that word to be found? Who knows how to discern and respond to God's authentic word? Is its authority self-evident, or does it strive for authority in the context of other forms and utterances?

When God's word sends forth its witnesses, how do they respond? How should they respond? What constitutes faithful and obedient service as ministry? What are the new frontiers? What are the fresh challenges? Is there a radically new spirituality that can reshape and transform their lives and their wills in these postmodern times? The chapters in this book attempt to offer some reflections on these important issues in the life of Christian ministry. We join with the psalmist in suggesting that the Word of God is like a lamp to our feet and a guide to our paths, and we trust that it will also be a strength to our lives, giving pep to our step and power to our feeble efforts.

Some of the material in this book formed parts of earlier presentations. For example, Chapters One, Four, and Five contain material delivered at the Virginia Theological Seminary in Alexandria, Virginia, as part of the Sprigg Lectures in 1992. Much of Chapter Eight formed part of the Convocation Lecture at the Howard University School of Divinity Annual Convocation in 1997. Some of the other material emerged from presentations to ecclesiastical gatherings, such as to the House of Bishops meeting of the Episcopal Church.

All of this shows, I hope, that these reflections have been long in germination, broad in application and deep in exploration. They are offered to a wider audience in the ecumenical community, with the firm conviction that those who are called to serve others in the name of Christ are also called to find their own nurture in Christ. Ministers of Christ, whether ordained or not, are to be sustained by a spirituality which is always in a lively and life-giving conversation with God's world. Such a conversation must be waged on many fronts and in many encounters with the strange and often complex modes of God's ongoing self-disclosures. It is principally by our openness to these encounters, guided by the convulsive fires of God's sustaining Spirit, that we shall be able to serve with power the very world into which God's Son was sent. When he came, he delivered the word and the people who heard him were astonished at his teaching, for he served his word with power (Lk 4:32). Why should we settle for less?

Kortright Davis
Howard University School Of Divinity
Washington, D.C.
September, 1998

CHAPTER ONE

CHRISTIAN
MINISTRY IN
CRISIS

"THE SOCIAL FABRIC IS BECOMING VISIBLY THINNER, our connections among one another are becoming visibly thinner. We don't trust one another as much, and we don't know one another as much. And, of course, that is behind the deterioration of the political dialogue, the deterioration of the public debate."[1] This claim was made by a Harvard University professor, Robert D. Putnam, in his attempt to blame television for the decline in American civil culture. He claimed that America's stock of social capital had seriously depleted since the 1930s with the advent of television. We must surely be in the throes of a great crisis when we find ourselves blaming inanimate objects, however compelling they might be, for the "thinning of our social fabric."

"Arrogance, greed, money and power are a combustible mixture in a legislative environment, and it finally exploded....My reaction was not one of surprise—we suspected this was going on. Gambling has dominated the legislature over the last four years. But I was shocked at the depth and breadth of what was revealed...."[2] These were the sentiments of a state senator from Louisiana, commenting on the alleged scandal surrounding the graft and corruption attributed to some legislators in that state. One legislator had reportedly joked about the situation in this way: "The good news is that the Tulane scholarship story is off the front page; the bad news is that because of the truck stop scandal, we're all going to jail."[3] There must surely be a moral crisis among our political directorate when they express no surprise about corruption, but instead try to make a joke out of it.

In the wake of several unpleasant episodes in the life of the Episcopal Church, such as the suicide of the late Bishop of Massachusetts, the reports of embezzlement, moral turpitude and other forms of corruption on the part of prominent church officials, many church members have been experiencing grave struggles of soul and spirit. For example, the former Presiding Bishop of the Episcopal Church, Edmond Browning, once reported that he felt "lonely, embattled, and immobilized" by the whole surge of recent events in his church, and their ripple effects. He spoke of having experienced the "dark night of the soul." "I saw everyone coming against me. I felt terribly abandoned.... You begin to look at all the slings and arrows pointed toward you and your paranoia rises to the highest height. You begin to question your own worth and purpose."[4] We must surely be in the throes of a serious ethical and spiritual crisis in the church when we feel free to throw slings and arrows at those who have not been found guilty of offending us.

When we read about the very young Roman Catholic bishop in Europe who resigned his office after publicly admitting that he had recently fathered a child by a young woman and had therefore broken his vow of celibacy, we were not particularly shocked by the report.

It seemed so *passe* to the ecclesiastical ear because such accounts of sexual exploits have more or less become commonplace. What was not normal, however, was the reason which the young prelate advanced for falling into the arms of his lover. He said that the pressures of being a bishop, and the stress of diocesan problems, had become so unbearable so quickly that he could only find solace and comfort in the companionship and affections of his lover. We must surely be in the throes of a great crisis of being human and religious at the same time, when we only become functional in our duties of sacred office with the aid of unholy alliances.

A recent profile of today's pastor in America has suggested that the three most stressful areas of a pastor's life are church politics, financial shortfall and difficult relationships with staff and other church officials. Other factors were personal and family illness, crises of personal faith, aging parents, death in the family and preparation for retirement. In all of these factors there appears to be little connection with the core of what the ministry is supposed to be about in the first place—the Gospel of Jesus Christ. The perils of preaching the Gospel are not connected with the Gospel itself. Rather, they reflect the cultural and material conditions under which the ministry of the Word has to be practiced. We must surely be in the throes of a crisis of ministry when the very context of ministry itself is heavily overlaid with countervailing circumstances and debilitating human forces.

Crisis in the society, crisis in the political culture, crisis in the ecclesial culture, crisis in the midst of preaching the Word: all these would seem to spell for us a certain sense of cynicism and despair. Yet we know that the meaning and thrust of the Gospel of Jesus Christ is symbolized in a cross, which is essentially a meeting point of confrontation and contradiction, of endless controversy and painful commitment. Is this what is meant by "a crisis of faith"? Let us see what this means for Christian ministry as a whole.

Is ministry in crisis? Who cares? To pose such a question is to invite some measure of concern, mixed perhaps with curiosity, contempt, and a reasonable dash of cynicism. Whose ministry are we talking about? Whose crisis are we pointing to? My grandmother would often remind me that what was "joke" for one was "death" for another. "Crisis" for one sector of society can often mean "moment of glory" for another. The second part of the question, "Who cares?" can either be taken as rhetorical or it can demand a serious answer.

Let us look at some of the contours of the contemporary crisis which exist at the intersection between the church-in-the-world and the world-of-the-church and explore what it means to live at this intersection—what it means to live with critical decisions. For the world of crisis is always a world of decisions, and the critical nerve is struck not so much by *what* we decide, but by *how* we decide it in our efforts to be servants or ministers with Christ.

Living with Crisis

Every generation in human history has lived with some crisis or another. Many have lived with the basic underlying notion that life itself is a crisis. We are told that the crisis of survival was so much a pivotal part of early human existence that most of daily life was spent in hunting for the means of sustenance. To hunt was to live, and to live was to hunt. Today, even if we have mastered much of the art of survival, we are still far from knowing what to do with the fruits of the survival we enjoy. The quality of life today is burdened not so much by problems of having or not having, but by problems of becoming, and the threat of meaninglessness. The great rush to spend more time on leisure has not produced any significant improvement in the quality of life for those who have more work-free time to spend. Boredom has overtaken work, home, marriages, power plays and even sports.

The Bible is quite consistent in associating moments of crisis with the formative epochs of our salvation history. The creation stories in Genesis begin with light being formed out of the chaos of the darkness which moved on the face of the waters. God's creative act begins in crisis. The Exodus story is preconditioned by the crisis of intransigence on the part of Egypt's Pharaoh who refuses to let God's people go. Suppose he had readily agreed to Moses' demands? What would have happened at the crossing of the Red Sea? The Passion narratives about Jesus in the gospel require the treachery of Judas, the conspiracy of the Jewish establishment and the complicity of Roman authorities. One recent film included a significant line in its script which suggests that Judas is to be given credit for the fact that Jesus is still playing to packed houses today. Suppose Jesus had been strategically ignored by his adversaries? What would we have substituted for the drama of the cross? The crisis in the New Testament churches is characterized by at least four main factors: the expectation of the imminent return of Christ, the backlash of popular Judaism, the attractiveness of other religious movements and the threat of extinction by Roman imperial policy. We cannot read the New Testament intelligently without hearing these echoes somewhere in the background.

The history of the Christian church is surely a story of one crisis after another. Persecution always produced expansion. That is why, in historical terms, we still speak of the blood of the martyrs as the seed of the church. The stoning of Stephen actually signaled the further edification of the nascent church of Jesus the Crucified One. The stones were turned into building blocks, as it were. Saul of Tarsus, who "consented" to Stephen's death, became the leading protagonist of the very gospel he had sought to extinguish. The shattering of the church always generated the scattering of the church. Crises of error and dissent often helped to stimulate the development and refinement of the *regula fidei,* the rule of faith. The Councils of Nicaea, Constantinople, Ephesus, and Chalcedon (between 325 and 451), to which we give historical pride of place in the formation of Christian doctrine, were more crisis-fighting moments than document-producing assemblies. Many of those who attended them did so with daggers in their hearts, if not actually in their hands. Such gatherings in the name of the church were thus not too far removed from many ecclesiastical conventions today. Theological and ideological daggers still abound in many of our church assemblies, and sectarian interests strongly compete with the light of the gospel and the warmth of God's transforming Spirit.

The history of the countless religious reformations is replete with accounts of crises upon crises. The formation of the black church as an institution in America, for example, was occasioned by a crisis of integrity among the Methodists in St. George's Church, Philadelphia, in 1787. This was in the context of the persistent and insatiable demands of white racism and its attendant doctrine of white supremacy. We must never forget that Richard Allen and Absalom Jones walked out of a church which had recently benefitted from their labors and their financial contributions as well as those of their fellow blacks. The emergence and evolution of the black church, as a distinct institution among American Christians, has to remain, in one sense, a permanent mark of crisis in American religion, for the conditions which created it then are still very much alive and well today.

As long as blacks generally remain unwelcome in the pews, the pulpits, the rectories, and pastors' manses, or at the altars of white churches, American Christianity is still very much in crisis. There can be no denying that American Christianity is produced and sustained by American economic and cultural history, a history that has been imprisoned by race and fueled by material profit. Professor Andrew Hacker writes: "A nation that has done so much to stress racial divisions should not be surprised if the result is not compassion and fellow feeling, but withdrawal and recrimination."[5]

What does it mean to live with each other's crises? For example, does the fact that persons are not Baptists or Roman Catholics render them immune from the critical issues that challenge those churches today? Or is it still true that if one member of the Body suffers, all suffer? I believe this to be the case, and that it would help us greatly if we could briefly explore a number of crises with which the church, as the living, breathing, feeling, and bleeding Body of Christ, is undoubtedly confronted at this time. Let's take a brief look at what I consider to be seven current areas of crisis in the church as a whole.

First, there is an ongoing struggle and search by the church for its own *sense of identity* in the modern world. Quite apart from the internal denominational squabbles about polity, ethos, resources, priorities, and theologies, there are also the interdenominational efforts to find a credible voice of moral and spiritual authority in the public sphere. The external pressures on the church to endorse social and political movements are often reinforced by internal machinations to pursue sectarian interests. The behavior of many who classify themselves as the "religious right," all in the name of Jesus and the flag, often leaves much to be desired in the cause of justice, social compassion or human equity. In the process, the church forgets that it is called to be the church. Francis Schüssler Fiorenza has rightly affirmed: "The church is more than a lobbying group, more than an agent of social welfare. It has a distinctive religious identity, and if it is to be the church, its religious identity must come to the fore in its style of commitment to social justice and in its commitment to human liberation."[6] There can hardly be any doubt that the church, in its current attempt to make itself more visible in the world, has become less capable of discerning its own identity. It seeks unwittingly to be given a fresh identity and role by the powers of secular rule and authority. At the very least, it seeks to have its identity validated by the explicit approval of those who care little for it. Whether the dominant image is that of Caesar's palace, or Pharaoh's court, the church in various and subtle ways still seeks its point of social reference and cultural identity from such sources, often oblivious of its rightful place at the heavenly throne of grace.

Second, there is a crisis of *spiritual sclerosis* in the church. There comes a time in the history of civilizations when movements for social change, revolutions in institutional arrangements, and the dissolution of codes of human conduct converge to challenge the very fabric of human stability. At such times the basic values of human maturity and moral courage normally combine to create a new character sufficient to meet the challenges of the new moment. Yet these values do not combine all by themselves. They are generally held together by a cultural substream and spiritual fervor which religion specifically can provide. Spiritual sclerosis is in evidence where the religious institutions, in addition to obscuring their religious identity, fail to provide spiritual reinforcement and nurture for their own members as well as for those who seek them out. For where the spirituality that is offered provides hardly more than a means of accepting the dominant social norms and values, regardless of their moral worth, then sclerosis has already set in. When the spirituality that is practiced in the church prepares its membership to adjust more comfortably to the public sphere, without any critical engagement or ethical consciousness based on faith in Jesus Christ as Lord, then spiritual sclerosis is already on the way. The hardening of the arteries (*sclerosis*) in the ecclesial body may not be sufficient to impede the flow of spiritual grace throughout the Body of Christ, but it certainly makes it difficult for Christian spirituality to function effectively in the world at large.

The third crisis follows from that which we have just mentioned. Let's call it *sacramental amnesia*. Sclerosis in prayer, in religious experience, in the genuine belief in the spiritual vitality of life in God, is further affected by the gradual process of desacramentalization in the church. The belief in God as creator has always made it possible for Christians to accept the inherent sacramentality in creation itself, as well as in the ongoing creative activity of God. A sacrament is an outward and visible sign of inward and spiritual grace. The acceptance of the sacramental nature of creation has drawn heavily on the doctrine of the resurrection, on the belief in the efficacy of God's grace, as well as on the sustained indwelling of God as Spirit. The sacramental life of creation has often been enhanced by the sacramental life in the church. The church is indeed God's major sacrament in the world. There are outward and visible signs of God's ongoing inward and spiritual grace. But amnesia has set in, for scientific pragmatism and technological rationalism have forced their way into the religious understanding of God's relationship with God's people.

The church has increasingly forgotten its stewardship of

the sacramental life. Instead, it has moved naively in its search for more instant and practical results, while unwittingly relegating such sacramental ministries as reconciliation and healing to forms of cynical neglect and spiritual indifference, or even to professional marketeers. Some Christian pastors prefer to be regarded as scientific counselors rather than as spiritual partners in human suffering and the struggle with Christian morality. The mysterious dimension in our human existence does not always provide observable signs of its vitality, but it is a viable reality nevertheless, full of meaning and spiritual force, and real worth. Increased sacramental amnesia tends to preclude us from the patient acceptance of such truths. Our scientific culture often forces us to become cynical toward that which is beyond our immediate grasp and comprehension. We forget that there is so much to us that will never meet the eye, so much that actually surpasses our human understanding, but nevertheless is still very real. There is a sacramentality in our human existence which we would do well to embrace, both as persons of faith and as a fellowship of believers in the availability of God's free and unmerited grace.

The *politics of sexuality* is the fourth area of crisis facing today's church. It constitutes perhaps one of the most emotional issues with which the Western church has had to deal for quite a long time. Not only does it place emphasis on who is called by God to be ordained (with all the theological gymnastics which modern church-persons have advanced throughout that debate), but it also brings the church right up against the meaning of human life itself. It touches on the procreation of children. It touches on the rights of adults in the choices they must make in the use of their human endowments. It impacts the social status of human relationships, as well as the rights of individuals to their own forms of self-expression. Questions concerning sexuality are as much a part of the politics of the church today as are questions of human rights or the privileges of unwed parents.

Central to all of this is the theology of the body. The body is our place in creation, that point of divine-human communication and encounter, that wonderful sacramental gift of God, that instrument of salvation, that living source of spiritual transcendence. That the human body has become a focal point of political and theological entanglement in the church is the major source of pain in this crisis today. No participant in the crisis can exist without a body; neither can anyone ever place himself or herself at the center of another's bodily existence. The politics of sexuality is creating one of the most pernicious distractions in the life of the church today. It presents every right-thinking Christian with major decisions about Christian values and human privacy, social tolerance and mutual acceptance, God's unconditional creative and forgiving love, and our own inclinations to place conditions on that love. In short, many would rather do the speaking for God in these matters, than to allow God to speak in God's own good time, and in God's own way.

Our fifth crisis area is that of *socio-cultural anemia.* This has to do with the realities of catholicity, or universality, in the church as a global community. The results of modern communications, global travel, and scientific collaboration have made it possible for various classes of members to share in the full life of the church. The rich diversity of cultures, the pluriformity of styles and symbols, the multiplicity of tones and accents, have all made it mandatory for us to set God free from any dominant cultural bondage. Imagine what joy there must be in the presence of God's angels on earth when people discover that God is neither white, male, nor English! Yet just at the time when the church should be in a position to benefit immeasurably from the rich diversity in the human family, it begins to suffer from socio-cultural anemia and finds it increasingly difficult to cope with varieties of cultures on a basis of mutuality, lively respect and common dignity. The church seems to persist in the dominant notion that some cultural traditions have greater divine sanction than others.

Political tokenism and benign neglect of cultural differences in the church often predominate, and the challenges of cultural pluralism are resisted as if they were signs of the Antichrist in some latter-day apocalyptic scenario. Even evangelistic campaigns for church growth, or revival missions for spiritual renewal, are carefully controlled so that the "wrong" people are not lured into joining the "wrong" churches. The doors of the church may be opened after the rousing sermon from the pulpit, but the ushers know that criteria for admission are still to be applied! It seems to me that the church that refuses to transcend culture and prejudice in its policies and practices and that refuses to strive relentlessly to affirm and transform them, is already paralyzed by socio-cultural anemia. The thrust for homogeneity in our churches, or for the preservation of cultural comfort zones in our congregations, may well be a serious indictment against what we claim to be all about. For the God who creates in diversity and sends us out to preach the gospel to all the world does not place restrictions on the types of candidates who are to be eligible for fellowship among us. Thus, in an increasingly pluralistic society, it is incumbent on the people of God to check and recheck all their prejudices at the doors of their churches, so that the strange census of the first Pentecost experience—Parthians, Medes, Elamites, Cretians, Arabians, dwellers of Mesopotamia, all speaking the wonderful works of God—does not become for our modern-day Christianity a source of social contradiction, rather than a bastion of religious conviction.

The sixth crisis is that of *structural fatigue.* Apart from the growing inability of most segments of the church to maintain their inherited material and physical structures, at least in their former glory, there is also a growing inability to sustain the religious and organizational traditions that have so far characterized the church's life. This ranges from such critical issues as the decline in membership, the dominance of professionalism over sacrificial vocation, the decline in the number of vocations to the ordained ministry and the religious life, the collapse of many ideological and theological support systems, to the decline of missionary enterprises, diminishing budgets, and the decreasing support for ecclesiastical organizations. The fatigue is perhaps nowhere more in evidence than in the graying of the official leadership in most church bodies, accompanied by a patent reluctance on its part to share power with younger generations. The instinct to protect ecclesiastical turf reflects the fear of many to hand over power; thus the church is faced with the prospect of structural transformation by attrition rather than by contrition.

The seventh area of crisis is that of an *authority malaise.* Not only is there increasing evidence that the church's spiritual and moral authority is being treated with contempt from within, but there is also painful testimony that the church's authority as a social and moral force is being ignored from without. Quite apart from the rapid decline in church attendance in Europe, and the proliferation of religious cults in North America, there is a growing sense of what is being referred to as the "evaporation of Christianity" in places where it once mattered.

This malaise was conspicuously in evidence during the events leading up to the war in the Persian Gulf. For months before the declaration of war on January 16, 1991, various church bodies held organized meetings, compiled documents, issued statements, sent telegrams, joined in marches, all in search of an alternative to open warfare. But *The Washington Post* could only make this assessment some two weeks after war broke out:

> The day before the United States led the first air attacks on Baghdad, mainly Protestant leaders called on the same principles—proportionality and last resort—in beseeching President Bush to delay military action. In the end, all of the letters, statements and reasoned arguments had no effect on the administration's determination to wage war, nor did the religious leaders issue a prohibition against fighting in the war that they had declared was unjust.[7]

Such a comment from a powerful medium in our society is painfully matched by the lived-out commentary which the membership of the church often makes by its modes of feeble witness. Does the church really take itself seriously? Does its membership take into account the norms and values which it seeks to espouse for the common good? This is the critical question for the authority of the church. Robert Bellah and his colleagues have offered this comment in their book *The Good Society:*

> The issue, both for the local parish and for the national or international church, is whether membership is accepted as having a formative claim on one's very sense of self, as involving a loyalty that can persist through difficulties, or whether membership is merely instrumental to individual self-fulfillment and, like some current conceptions of marriage, can be abandoned as soon as it 'doesn't meet my needs'.[8]

This comment is of considerable significance for our discussion, for it is central to our understanding of a Christian ministry that is based on **discipleship** rather than on **membership**.

These seven areas of crisis which we have been discussing do not by any means exhaust the list of concerns in our contemporary scene. They merely serve to point us in a certain direction, toward the maze of crises in which we are called to be followers of Christ. It is the critical question of the call to discipleship that must always inform any discussion of the ministry, and to this we now turn our attention.

Call and Crisis

Foundational to our faith as Christians is the claim that the God who calls the world into being is the God who called Abraham away from his native land. Our biblical tradition asserts that the God who called Abraham away also sent Moses back into Egypt, Amos up to Samaria, Jesus into Jerusalem, and Saul of Tarsus into Damascus. This is a God who is always calling and sending. This is the God who calls the church into being. This is why the church is the *ecclesia,* the community of those who have been called out, called together, called upwards to a higher order of being, in order to become the living sign of the Realm of God. The Realm of God is already on the way through the faithful response of those who share in the new life of Christ. This sharing in the new life of Christ through baptism involves a new character freely made available to us, defined neither by historical accidents nor by social circumstances.

Paul's proclamation about the ministry of reconciliation is prefaced by a very important discussion on the meaning of our new Christian reality, the "in Christ" reality. This is what he says: "And he died for all, that those who live might live no longer for themselves but for him who for their sake died and was raised. From now on, therefore, we regard no one from a human point of view; even though we once regarded Christ from a human point of view, we regard him thus no longer. Therefore, if any one is in Christ, he is a new creation; the old has passed away, behold, the new has come" (2 Cor 5:15–17).

Just as the old creation takes place out of the crisis of chaos and darkness, so does the new creation take place out of the crisis of alienation and disobedience. That is why Paul can refer to God's work, to Christ's life and ministry, and to his own ministry as the ministry of reconciliation. God gave us the ministry of reconciliation, he says, by our being reconciled to God. God has entrusted to us the message of reconciliation and appointed us as ambassadors of Christ, through whom the whole operation has been taking place. Paul knows of no discontinuity between the call, the character, the commission and the community. The community that God calls into being is therefore a community that seeks to respond faithfully to that God. It is not a community that calls out arrogantly. The nature of the response to that call is always that which seeks to embody the realities and challenges of reconciliation.

This tells us in no uncertain terms what discipleship is all about. It is about responding to the call of Christ to follow him. It is a call that is never abrogated by any other responsibility to which the disciple may happen to be summoned. Stanley Hauerwas of Duke University has rightly stated that: "We are not Christians because of what we believe, but because we have been called to be disciples of Jesus. To become a disciple is not a matter of a new or changed self-understanding, but rather to become part of

a different community with a different set of practices."[9]
The community of disciples is the community of the Spirit,
the spiritual community, and as many as are led by the
Spirit of God are children of God, says Paul. The inextricable connection between discipleship and filial relationship
with God is assured by the presence of the Spirit of God.
Through the Spirit, the disciple can address God as Jesus
addresses God, "Abba," "Daddy." This is not just teddy
bear talk, it is real baby-talk. For unless we are transformed and become as little children, we will not fit in
with the terms of the Realm of God. The words are not
mine; they come from the lips of Jesus himself.

What then is the nature of the crisis in ministry, as far
as God's call is concerned? It has to do with ordination,
and the critical role that it has played over the centuries
in the life and witness of the community of disciples. The
problem begins with Jesus himself who neither baptizes
anyone, nor ordains anyone. He himself is not ordained
either. He calls disciples to follow him, he shares with
them the mission that he has received from his Father. As
he leaves them for the last time, he sends them out to
make disciples as they preach the gospel. Apostleship is
incidental; discipleship is essential. Those who are sent do
not cease to be disciples. They are sent because they have
already responded to Jesus as disciples, and they are
expected to invite others to become as they are. There is a
missionary dimension in Christian discipleship that is to
be employed faithfully in the service of the Realm of God.

If Christian ministry and Christian discipleship are identical, then what do we do with the presumed call to ordination? Whose call is it? How does it relate to that re-
creative act of God in calling the church into being? How do
we know whom God calls into holy orders, and whom God
does not? To whom does God entrust such powers of discernment? Where do our tastes and styles, our prejudices

and fears and our power plays fit in? How do we distinguish whether the quest for ordination is an application for a job, a thirst for power, or a genuine response to God's call? Who else is to hear when God is calling an individual in the particularity of his or her own story?

The procedures for selecting candidates for ordination have generally been gravely visited by four highly undesirable trends in recent times. First, there has been the *politicization* of the process by the invasion of socio-political and ecclesiastical dynamics that bear no relationship to the demands of the gospel, nor to the wrenching urgings of the Spirit. The decision to accept a candidate for ordination in a church is often heavily overlaid with political considerations that have nothing whatsoever to do with divine vocation or divine commission. Because of this, we have often included some who ought not to have been, for reasons which frequently become too obvious after the deed has been done. And we have often excluded some whose call has been genuinely perceived but not articulated clearly enough for us to be sure.

Second, the process often seeks to reflect very faithfully the dominant ideology of those whose preferences and power must be satisfied at all costs. I call this the *ideologization* of the process. There is often a need for ideological correctness, theological compatibility with the dominant powers-that-be, or the perception of a social presence in the candidate that will enhance the prejudices and sectarian values of those who have the power to choose. In such circumstances, the church ends up getting the candidates it deserves, only because it entrusted the choice to the members it did not deserve. Thereafter, generations of its members have to live with such results in its clerical orders.

Third, there is the *psychologization* of the process, by which it often appears that the words of psychologists and psychoanalysts carry an inordinate amount of weight in the discernment process. They often seem to carry more weight than the word of theologians, or pastors, or faithful members of congregations who know good pastors when they see them, or who have a continuing sense of what is needed in their pastors. While their theological imperatives are often shrouded in mystery, commissions and boards on ministry seem to delight in functioning as amateur psychologists with a fascination for the absurd. Further, this factor says, "If you don't have a heartbreaking story, you don't have a chance." People who have not had many dramatic or sensational twists in their lives, but who have nurtured a sense of call from a very early age, are ushered away to search for some more exciting reasons to seek ordination. It cannot be, they seem to say, that God can call those with a Samuel-like experience to serve in the sacred orders of the ordained ministry. Vocation and traumatic bad luck seem to them to go hand in hand.

Fourth, there is the *Wheel of Fortune* factor. If you guess the right buzz-words you win; if you use your own words you lose. You must know the answers to the special catechism by heart. Or you must reflect in your examinations the kinds of issues that scratch the committee members exactly where they think they are itching. Or you must appropriate to yourself the kind of vision about mission, ministry, church, market, money, organizations, or even relationships, which arrest and hold the interests and fascination of the decision-makers. In the end, it often appears to be a game. You can win if you try hard enough, but the board members are there to have sacred fun at your expense. You need patience, perception, quick-wittedness, and lots of luck. If you don't have the right ticket, you don't have a chance! There are many hurdles to jump over, and jump you must!

These four factors are reinforced by a narrow vision of the Church of God on the part of many selectors. Quite often, ordination is narrowly understood in terms of a particular type of church or congregation, rather than in terms of the whole church. For example, in their pastoral letter, *But We See Jesus,* the black bishops of the Episcopal Church were very forthright in their assertion:

> We cannot ignore the deplorable fact that many commissions on ministry in our church are not necessarily the agencies for encouraging and helping aspirants of color towards ordination. Black aspirants have claimed that many of their encounters with diocesan hierarchies have been riddled with circumstances far removed from the noble values of charity, sensitivity, tolerance, patience, mutuality, or even fairness....If these claims be true, we resolutely deplore such developments, and we call on all our fellow bishops and their commissions to be as fair, open, honest and enabling as would more accurately indicate that there is justice in our church for all people of all races.[10]

The foregoing sentiments were very closely akin to what the black bishops of the Roman Catholic Church in this country had observed in their own pastoral letter, *What We Have Seen and Heard* (1984). The bishops called on their diocesan vocation directors to

> collaborate with leaders in the Black Catholic community in strategic planning for the recruitment of Black young men for the diocesan priesthood. The same planning and collaborative effort should be part of the vocational planning of the many religious congregations and seminaries. Care should be taken

to know and understand the attitudes and concerns of Black young people in order to show how ministry would be relevant to their lives and experience.[11]

The bishops went further and bemoaned that "regretfully, experience has shown that once inside a seminary, a novitiate or a house of formation many minority students face a period of cultural and social alienation."[12]

The Bishop's Committee on the Liturgy in the Roman Catholic Church (USA) has also made some comments about the evangelization of African Americans in their famous document *Plenty Good Room: The Spirit and Truth of African American Catholic Worship* (1991). In one very telling passage, the Committee refers to the fate of parishes in the Roman Catholic Church that underwent a transformation from white to black. They wrote:

> Whenever a parish changed from serving white Americans to serving African Americans, the ordinary policy of most dioceses was to turn parish administration over to religious orders that were willing to take up the special ministry to African Americans. One dubious result of this segregated ministry was that certain religious orders attracted a few African American vocations, while most diocesan seminaries and communities of religious women attracted almost none.[13]

There still appears to be the presumption in some places that God would never call a black man to be the pastor of a white congregation, although God seems to have been calling white men to lead black parishes for centuries. The agony of this crisis is felt by countless men and women, both black and non-black, throughout the church. It is a crisis that exists at the point of confrontation between

divine vocation and human prejudice. When some powerful Christians say no, not even God can say yes. Even if
God were to say yes, there would be no job for them any-
way!

Father Joseph Brown, S.J., of the Roman Catholic Church,
has recently made a strong call for a review of the treat-
ment of African American candidates for ordination. In
his very helpful book, *To Stand on the Rock,* Brown asserts
"A church come of age must steward its own institutions,
offering guidance, financial support, and political and
institutional protection, whenever possible and wherever
necessary."[14] He decries the current practices of seminary
training of African Americans which is provided "with the
goal of proving that the old demonizations of black men
and women are not true, most often by becoming *exceptions* to whatever stereotype may prevail. The great effort
to send African American men and women into seminaries, monasteries, and convents has been historically
directed as much as the goal of validating the religious
gifts of black Catholics as at supplying indigenous workers
in the African vineyards."[15]

Is ministry in crisis then? Yes, because ministry is continually equated with ordination rather than with discipleship. As long as we continue to speak and act in this
way, the whole nature of Christian vocation will be narrowly focused and gravely misunderstood. As long as ordination continues to be seen as elevation to power, rather
than the setting apart of disciples for special service on
behalf of the community of disciples, then terms of
Christian service with human endearment within the
church will continue to be gravely obscured. As long as
Christian ministry is seen as the prize to be grasped,
rather than as the life of Christ to be shared with others,
then the light of the cross shines no brighter than Pilate's
piercing spear.

I agree with Edward Schillebeeckx in his assertion: "The tension between an ontological-sacerdotalist view of the ministry on the one hand and a purely functionalist view on the other must therefore be resolved by a theological view of the church's ministry as a charismatic office, the service of leading the community, and therefore as an ecclesial function within the community and accepted by the community. Precisely in this way it is a gift of God."[16] Frank Allan once put it this way: "Ministry, of course, is not contingent upon ordination. Rather, one enters ministry when one enters the waters of baptism....Not only should we stop using the terms 'ministry' and 'ordination' synonymously, but we should also begin acting in a different way."[17] God's gift of ministry is identical with God's call to discipleship. We therefore need to consider the meaning of Christian ministry as discipleship, since the crises of the church and the captive nature of the ordained ministry create serious problems for those who simply seek to be persons of faith, rather than persons of power.

Ministry as Discipleship

Our sense of call to ministry finds its strongest means of fulfillment within the fellowship of the community of faith, the people of God, the Body of Christ. Ministry is always ministry in context; it possesses a nature that is inalienably corporate. Because Christian ministry is always corporate ministry, we dare not speak of a privatized ministry, even if God calls each of us in the particularity of our own personhood. It is precisely because ministry is corporate that it is understood to be also discipleship, for discipleship is always a corporate form of existence. Together we discover our followership of Jesus Christ. To quote Schillebeeckx again: "...the ministry of the church above all requires of its ministers leadership in the true discipleship of Jesus, with all the spirituality which this 'discipleship of Jesus' involves in New Testament terms."[18]

The theology of ministry and the theology of the church are thus inseparable. We do well to seek a fresh understanding of ministry as discipleship by once again taking another look at what we have traditionally referred to as the four marks of the church. Readers will no doubt recognize that I am very fond of taking my hermeneutical starting point from what the Nicene Creed says about the church to which we belong. We must never forget that the Creed also says that it is that church in which we believe. To use the confessional marks of the church as a paradigm for understanding our place and role in it, and through it, appears to me to be a very significant and rewarding exercise in any search for a new spirituality for ministry. We may not change the Creed. At least, we are not supposed to. We are expected to be faithful to what we profess, while searching for new ways of expressing and understanding what that Creed demands of us in our own day and time. Here, then, as in other sections of this book, an attempt will be made to further our theological explorations of some practical meanings of our belief in the "One, Holy, Catholic, and Apostolic Church." We speak of these as the four marks of Unity, Holiness, Catholicity, and Apostolicity.

First, when we speak of the *unity* of the church we are drawing on our primary understanding of the oneness of God—the single and unrepeatable nature of God's calling the church into being—as well as on our acceptance of that church as the One Body of Christ. The character of discipleship that springs from the unity of the church is that of integration—the constant discovery of a single identity in Christ. The disciple is called to **personal integration** and wholeness, to pursue that singleness of vision in which Christian heart and worldly treasure are not strangers to each other.

Second, we confess our faith in the *holy* church. We believe that the church is holy, because of the Holy Spirit's indwelling presence and activity of sanctification, consecration, enlightenment and divine guidance. The call to ministry as discipleship here is that of *personal consecration,* that relentless task to redeem every living moment for God, chiefly by affirming the sanctifying presence of God in every concrete situation.

Third, we are members of God's *catholic* church. Catholicity embraces many factors, chief among them being totality, universality, openness, freedom and classlessness. The call to ministry as discipleship is that of *personal liberation,* not liberalism. For while Christian liberation means to be set free by the gospel, liberalism is often the exchange of one form of intellectual bondage for another. Personal liberation through Christ knows only the call to transform, and the joy of being transformed.

Fourth, we believe in the *apostolic* church, the church that is sent, the community of faithful disciples who are only who they are because they are on the move. The apostolic church is the band of God's people moving forward, moving outward, moving upward, always away from themselves to be fully involved in God's mission. Movement is the soul of the church, for it is a pilgrim community, finding no resting place other than in God's perfect Realm. The call to ministry as discipleship is that of **personal animation,** a personal restlessness in the midst of moral, spiritual, and relational crises. The disciple is driven by God's Spirit to make no peace with oppression, to turn bad news into good by the power of the cross, and to demonstrate that *laborare* is truly *orare;* that is, to work is really to pray.

●

In sum, then, Christian ministry as Christian discipleship finds its basic character in the very nature of God's church. It is a call to personal integration, personal consecration, personal liberation, and personal animation. Henri Nouwen writes: "Ministry in a mystical sense involves an inner freedom that radiates and heals. It thereby means more what we are than what we do....We shouldn't worry so much about trying to influence and do good to each other, which, without rootedness in God, can end up being not real ministry but simply a way of dominating one another. Rather, we should concentrate on being faithful and obedient to God."[19]

Is ministry in crisis then? Who cares? God doesn't! In the fullness of time God sent a Son, not a minister, to redeem the world. Is ministry in crisis? Yes, but crisis often creates challenge, and change, and new character. If ministry is in crisis, who cares? Only those who would seek to cultivate ministry as power, status, self-service and personal mobility. But those who seek to respond to God's call to faithful discipleship, within the fellowship and followership of Christ, strive only to work out that ministry in terms of *servanting* and *friendship*. It is to such people that we will turn our attention in Chapters Four and Five. But we need to turn immediately to a discussion on some new frontiers for the Christian ministry.

CHAPTER TWO

NEW FRONTIERS FOR MINISTRY

WHAT DOES IT REALLY MEAN TO HAVE A LIVELY faith in God? What happens when this lively faith goes to work? Our lively faith in God is so empowered by the persistent fires of the Holy Spirit that we keep trying to discover those characteristics of the new creation which God is somehow making real through us in our own time. Not only is our faith a divine gift of constant discovery and discernment, but it is also a continuing mandate for our radical engagement in the actual, historical and concrete contexts of our lives.

This faith, which we share in common with other Christian believers, is often spoken of as a pilgrimage, a journey that never ends. But it always takes place in the light of that glorious end, which is already assured to us by the resurrection of Jesus Christ from the dead. The faith of the Christian is essentially a resurrection faith. It is always seeking with confidence for that which is above, that which is beyond. But resurrection faith is not only faith *on the rise,* it is also faith *on the move.* We move forward together as a community of believers, risen with Christ, and leaving behind as much as we can all the structures and vestiges of a slave-like mentality, or social entombment. For structures are made to be in service of the pilgrim community, the pilgrim community is not called to be in service of the structures. It is fitting, therefore, that as we are called by God into service, into ministry, we should be passionately concerned with the search for new frontiers in ministry, and not just with new patterns, or styles, or structures. Yet, no new awareness of ministry is possible without a renewed sense of obedience to God's call to mission.

What then are the frontiers for new ministry to which God may well be directing our attention at this time? We need to remember that frontiers are never of our own making; they are always part of the journey ahead of us. Further, we should also remember that we never have any control over what is likely to occur beyond the frontiers. Frontiers involve risk and the breaking of barriers. Frontiers call for the sharpening of resolve, and the ready willingness to face difficulties. Frontiers often demand the dissolution of prejudices, and a courageous openness to radical change. Frontiers offer possibilities and experiences that can only be seized by a radically new vision.

New frontiers always sound a warning that we can never be the same again. Our old friends may desert us. Our basic habits may be transformed. Our former strengths may be exposed for their hidden weakness. Our Jericho walls may fall. New life may emerge from our valleys of dry bones. New frontiers spell *kairos*—fresh moments of divine opportunity. God's rushing mighty wind, blowing relentlessly beyond our calculated control, may yet deliver new tongues, enabling us to speak afresh to the Parthians, Medes and Elamites of our day, of the wonderful works of God in the wonderful world of God. Nothing less than a new Pentecostal experience can empower us to do the scratching precisely at those points where the family of God is itching, both in the church and in the world. Three groups of frontiers seem to me to suggest themselves: *Frontiers in Ministry, Frontiers for Service, Frontiers in Mission.* We shall look at each in turn.

Frontiers in Ministry

Within this group we should obviously begin with the very question which must have occupied the mind of God at the time of Isaiah. In the face of the historical crisis with which the people of Israel are confronted in the prophet's day, God is not seized by the *what*. God is primarily concerned with the *who*. The quality of the minister, or the prophet, is more critical than the apparent urgency of the task: "Whom shall I send?" This is the heavenly question. Oddly enough, today we tend to be overwhelmed by a plethora of earthly responses: "Here we are, send us!" There is certainly no shortage of ministers today, but there is also no scarcity of ministerial burn-out or pastoral fatigue. Divine vocation is blurred by patterns of sacred scheming, to which we alluded in our previous chapter. The primacy of sacrifice is supplanted by the urgency for gain. The power of the Word is held hostage by the words of the powerful. Surely, in the midst of all of this, God must be beckoning the whole church to new frontiers in ministry, to a ministry which belongs to the whole people of God and not solely to those set apart by ordination or institutional recognition.

Five frontiers suggest themselves. First, there is the question of *ministry to the ministers.* Who ministers to the ministers? I am particularly concerned about bishops, presiding elders, superintendent ministers and other chief pastors among us. Who feeds the shepherds and those who are charged to feed the under-shepherds of the flock of Christ? We have tended to function as if they have an interminable supply of grace and professional strength to cope with the problems of pastoral leadership. Bishops and their counterparts are essentially pastors of pastors, and if they are not properly fed, the pastors they lead will also suffer from grave spiritual and pastoral malnourishment. We have obviously taken the needs of the leaders of our churches for granted for too long, and we have been caught by surprise when crises and pockets of turbulence have erupted among them. The church's ministry to its chief pastors is just as important as the ministry of the chief pastors to the church. The endemic loneliness and thanklessness of high clerical office should never be augmented by ecclesiastical negligence, or organizational anemia. If we, as God's people, feed our chief pastors well, we may yet prevent their being fed to God's people later on.

The second frontier has to do with the nature and formation of what I call the *ecclesial character*. There must be something in the inherent nature of the Christian which sets him or her apart as a member of the church of God, a follower of Jesus Christ and a bearer of the good news of the Realm of God. I am not sure how to describe it, but it must be there in such strength and authenticity that it cuts across all of our cultural, ethnic and other inherited antecedents. Such a character has little to do with any particular denominational ethos, or social identity. Is there not a specific kind of character that Jesus envisaged for his faithful followers? Were there not repeated episodes in his ministry in which he was at pains to stress that certain factors were expected in the normal character of those who had decided to follow him? If, in our theology, we are at pains to stress the indelibility of ordination, we should be even more anxious to stress the indelibility of an ecclesial character for the priesthood of all believers, conferred on us by baptism.

What does this mean in effect? It means that not only is the presumed dichotomy between the ordained and lay character cancerous to the spiritual life of our church (did Jesus not emancipate us from the tyranny of clericalism once and for all?), but the assimilation of church life and practice to secularized norms and values, especially in the fields of psychology and political science, is scattering the flock for whom Jesus Christ gave his life. We need to develop intensive programs of ecclesial character formation through which the common heritage of our baptismal character can be constantly assessed in the light of prevailing contexts, and by which the distinctive factors of our Christian calling can be fervently renewed. Let the church be the church, and nothing but the church.

Our third frontier in this category has to do with the *ministry to the strong.* How do we minister to the strong? It is so easy to minister to the weak, the poor, the helpless and destitute, the marginalized and the oppressed, the broken and the lonely. Indeed, we seem to find it impossible to minister to those who do not seem to have any such problems. There must be a problem lurking around somewhere, we think, and we will browse around until it appears; only then can we minister. Christian ministry is too often caricatured as a leveling off, rather than as a reaching out, whether up or down. The modern church is full of many strong people—actually, not metaphorically, strong—who yearn to have their need for God adequately met at their own level of existence. It is a travesty of the gospel to deal with them as if they were spiritually weak or to demand that they recondition themselves before pastoral services are rendered. But perhaps only the strong should minister to the strong. The encounter of Jesus with the rich young ruler was not about impoverishment and weakening, it was about the rearrangement of priorities and the hierarchy of responsibilities. An appropriate ministry to the strong in our midst is an urgent task on the new frontiers of ministry, and it will not be addressed either by an obsequious mentality, or by an arrogant spirituality. Strong people are God's holy people also.

Our fourth frontier is another area of strength in the church that we frequently overlook. Long ago, Jesus used the paradigm of the child to remind his hearers about the means of entry into the Realm of God. "Except you become as little children, you cannot enter the kingdom of God," he said. *Children are still the most authentic carriers of what we mean by the image of God.* They stick closer to the paths of truth, justice and humanity. They bring joy and hope to our faith community. They provide us with a reason for working hard.

Yet we often do not listen to the messages they bring us from God. Our concern for the children of our churches should not be merely about their future; we should also be concerned about receiving their ministry to us in the here and now. God has much to teach us through our children, and we need to be honest enough to discern what they can do for us, rather than to concentrate solely on what we can do for them. I want to suggest that there is such a thing as a "paedeographic theology"—that is, a theology crafted by children, and the innocence of their vision which can emancipate us from the shackles of our own adult obsolescence. The new Word from the Lord is coming faithfully and forcefully from the lips of our children.

The fifth frontier is about *reclaiming God's people.* We have become accustomed to the fact that church statistics often fluctuate, and that we should do little more than doubt their accuracy. Nevertheless we need to remember that each statistic represents a person, and that those who are no longer with us as members are still the persons for whom Christ died. We need to go after the "no-more" Christians, those who have left the church entirely.

A special type of evangelism is indicated here as we seek to reclaim God's people for God. Such efforts demand risk, courage and imagination. They also require a radical rearrangement of our modes of hospitality, as well as a warm, welcoming, and humble manner on the part of our clergy. For better or for worse, the clergy are still the walking billboards of our churches.

Frontiers for Service

Within this second range of insights, we should draw attention to some new possibilities for service. The notion of service here, however, has more to do with *leitourgia,* that is, with the ongoing work and operation of the church as church, rather than with *diakonia,* or the ministry of service. God has called the church into being so that God's *diakonoi,* God's servants, can be exercised continuously in God's *leitourgia* in God's world. We will no doubt recognize that we get the word "liturgy" from *leitourgia.* The church does liturgy not only through its prayer books and worship services but also through the world of common living. The worshipping church may be the most conspicuous sign that the church exists, but *only* the church that seeks to bear witness that what it really believes is true to itself and its mission. Only such a church can authentically make the claim that God really does exist. How then can a church at worship guarantee that it does not turn in on itself by self-adulation and earthbound piety? It can do so by exploring new frontiers of faithful service in the light of the gospel it proclaims through Word and Sacrament, Work and Witness. Five frontiers suggest themselves.

First, *the structures by which we conduct our affairs in the church* need to be reassessed. The principal criterion by which we evaluate success or failure in the proclamation of the gospel and the management of our life together, as a community of faith, is heavily overlaid with values which are antithetical to the Realm of God. Even the priorities we set for selecting our church officers or postulants for ministry often call into question the grace of God's foolishness, as St. Paul understood it. We have already discussed the process of selection of candidates for ordination in our previous chapter. Although we are challenged by Jesus about the wisdom of the children of this world, in contrast to the children of light, we are prone to be more submissive to the scientific norms of secular business than we are to exemplifying the godly values of Christian practice. Christian structures are always to be characterized by the cross as the symbol of risk, love, humility and yielding. Bishops, for example (who often wear pectoral crosses), must strive to be pastors of pastors, rather than hard-nosed executives driven by the heartlessness of presumed objectivity or the blistering coldness of modern bureaucracy. The finest bishops and chief pastors in our churches are not always among the "best" administrators, by secular standards. But what shall it profit any chief pastor to gain the whole world but lose touch with the very soul of the flock? Many of our ecclesiastical structures appear to stand in dire need of some spiritual, moral, humane, and theological reinforcement, so that we might once again flourish in the business of losing to the flesh while gaining to the Spirit. We need the grace, the wisdom and the courage to become businesslike without becoming a business. The New Testament word for this is prudence (*phronesis*), not profit.

Second, there is the question of *stewardship*. This is a popular issue throughout the church, as we seek to mobilize available resources for the preferred work of church bodies. Various configurations of the meaning of "tithe" are already in place, and there are specialists at work who produce the magical formulae for miraculous results. Yet so much of this activity is alien to the spirit of the first ecclesial community we encounter in the Acts of the Apostles. The earliest church understood itself to be essentially a community of needs, rather than a community of goods and services. It was therefore prepared to transform itself into a sacrificial community, a community of sharing, a community in which the members cared enough for each other so as to enter into the poverty of each other. Christian fellowship demanded the sharing of poverty and pain as a precondition for the sharing of wealth and resources. The new frontier for our church today is to seek the dethronement of the primacy of economic wealth in a context of material prosperity, and to enter sacrificially into the sharing of each other's poverty in practical and concrete ways. The life of the Christian must no longer consist in the abundance of the things which he or she possesses, for the camels seem to be passing through the eye of the needle much faster than we seem to be reaching our professed destination of the Realm of God.

Our third frontier in this section has to do with *the liturgy of the church*. While it is difficult to determine what areas require renewal, it is not so difficult to recognize that most of our liturgical activity represents a secure retreat from the world and its challenges, or sometimes a sacred antidote to the threats of secular advances. We cannot offer our corporate worship to the God who takes the world seriously, while attempting to sanitize ourselves from the smell of the world or the cries of those trapped in its snares. Every liturgy is a political event. It brings together a group of like-minded people who share a common confession of faith, and who make a sacramental act in the face of an anti-sacramental culture. We claim that there is more to us than meets the eye, but our secular culture claims that there is not. Liturgy always takes place in an alien context, in the midst of a desacralizing world. The new frontier for us here is to develop ways in which our liturgies can incorporate more effectively the daily cares, experiences, and expectations of God's liberating work in the world, as well as the management of our time and talents in that direction. I believe that God, the Enlivening Spirit, is directing us toward a much closer co-identification of the broken bodies in the streets and ghettos of our world with the breaking of Christ's body on the altars in our churches.

This brings us to our fourth frontier—*the nature of the congregation itself.* Generally speaking, congregations often resolve themselves into religious groups. They tend to function like theaters, or corporations, or social organizations, country clubs, or even multi-purpose hospitals. Most national constitutions guarantee religious rights and freedoms, but there is a higher constitution in the gospel which makes far more significant demands. However much church membership fulfills one of our social needs, we are never to be enlisted just for the fun of it. Perhaps the image of the fun-loving, coffee or cocktail-drinking, self-promoting, esoteric, prim-and-proper Christian congregation is exhausting itself.

The new frontier represents a radically new context: a selfless, simple, servantlike, and emancipatory company of witnesses that needs to emerge. Our congregations must be transformed. The self-serving gimmickry must cease. The quests for entertainment and fun in our churches must be replaced by a critical sense of urgency to serve the poor and the needy. I do not understand the footwashing mandate of Jesus in any other way. Such a mandate cannot simply be relegated to the status of a liturgical extra on Maundy Thursday night. Every congregation must be an agent of Christ, where the footwashing business that he started is carried on without fear or compromise. We must discover new modes of nurture in and through our congregations that will inspire dynamic ways of becoming faithful servants, rather than devising subtle ways of being served by others.

What about our human prejudices? Do we seek to have them baptized, confirmed, ordained and canonized? Does God seek to sanction our fixed positions? Or is there not in us a constant quest to preserve ourselves and our identity from being invaded by those who are different from us? Our fifth frontier is *to struggle systematically for the goal in our common life when "different" will no longer mean "inferior."* Our modern ethos warmly accommodates itself to the convenient divisions of congregations on the basis of race, class, geography and wealth. It treats with some suspicion efforts at developing pluralistic memberships. Cultural and racial integration is an option that often lacks wide acceptance. We dare not presume to worship a saving God who neglects to save us from our deepest prejudices. We dare not treat our ethnic heritage as being so precious and divine as to exclude the ethnic heritage of others who are different from ourselves. Even if we are tempted to believe that ethnic diversity is sufficient ground for human division, we should be honest enough to recognize that God's creative act of diversity has been followed up by God's re-creative act of unity. Thus the opposite of an integrated congregation is not a segregated, but a disintegrated one. The spiritual and cultural resistance to integrated congregational life is perhaps the strongest manifestation of the need for God's fresh emancipation in our churches today.

Frontiers in Mission

We come then to our third range of frontiers. They deal essentially with the meaning of *kerygma,* or proclamation,

as one of the basic tasks of the church. We are reminded
continually that we are sent out into the world to preach
the gospel to all the nations, and to baptize them in the
name of God. This is the God whom we experience as the
solidness of love. That is what we mean by the traditional
doctrine of the Trinity. The affirmation of God as Creator,
Redeemer, and Sanctifier (or Father, Son, and Holy Spirit),
God as the Holy and Blessed Trinity, is not merely for our
liturgical doxology—it is also for our implementation in the
world. The Great Commission in Matthew 28 is that we
should put our belief in the trinitarian God to work in God's
world. Thus *kerygma* is more about *what we do,* and not
merely about *what we say.* The frontiers in mission therefore
beckon us beyond the borders of our church and into the
arena of many diverse realities, risks and enterprises, on to
the cutting edge of God's ongoing creative activity.

First, we are beckoned to engage more truthfully and
fearlessly in *the sphere of ecumenism.* We should never be
accused of praying frequently for ecumenism, that all may
be one in Christ, then doing less and less to achieve it.
There is a widespread suspicion that most mainline
denominations are really anti-ecumenical, regardless of
the rhetoric and highly visible events they often sponsor.
We need to break new ground in ecumenical ventures, not
just in friendly dialogue with like-minded groups, but also
in fertile solidarity with other groups (religious and non-
religious) which share a passionate concern for the development of full humanity and justice in our day. Christian
unity involves the unity of the whole human family, and
we dare not settle for offering up to God our preference
for a family within a family. God's *oikoumene* extends
beyond the church, and we need to explore with honesty
and trusting faith what it means to work for the coming
of the Realm of God, for which we pray daily in the Lord's
Prayer.

The second frontier is that of *reconstructing ethical structures in our society*. We have become accustomed to accepting the historical judgment that we are living in a post-Christian age. Some refer to it as the postmodern age. What does this mean for our standards of Christian conduct, our sense of moral duty, or the structures of spiritual response to the realities of our day? What are we to teach our children? What makes right things right, or wrong things wrong? How do we teach them to do the right thing in the right way? We have been working against nuclear bombs, racism, homophobia, sexism and ethnocentrism. And we do well. Do we not need to go into the sanctuaries of corporate America and Hollywood, the world of sports, medicine, and academia, to wrestle for the future of our children in these vital areas which are already affecting both our lives and theirs?

Allied to this is our third frontier dealing with *technology*. We should indeed be justly proud that we have achieved so much in the field of technological advance. We have conquered the moon. We have computerized our way of life to such an extent that we no longer trust any other system of determination. Our whole personhood can now be represented by a computer printout. We are indeed living under the tyranny of technocracy. Technology governs our thinking and literally shapes our lives. What kind of spirituality do we need for counteracting, or at least coping more effectively with, these advances? How can we help those left behind by this relentless surge of technology? How can we be simply human—with feeling, passion, pain, joy, failure—and try again? The grace of God gives us a second chance, but the force of technology does not. The new frontier of technological spirituality demands that we as the church engage the world in a battle for its soul, so that we strive to witness to our basic faith that *technology was made for humanity and not humanity for technology*. There must surely be limits to growth, and we must not be afraid to establish them today for tomorrow might be too late.

There is also the field of development—social, economic, and human development. We have gone through four so-called developmental decades in which we have made claims that we have been helping the poor to help themselves. Yet the results have come in, and they now show that the reverse has happened. The gap between rich and poor has widened. The nature of absolute poverty in the world has worsened. The transfer of resources on the global scale has actually moved from the poor countries to the rich. Christians in the rich developed world have been overcome by compassion fatigue. They no longer care how the other half of the world lives. Underdevelopment is partly of our own making. We cannot afford to grow weary in the business of caring for the less fortunate members of our planet, or in sharing the bounties of our wealth and talents with our brothers and sisters in the rest of the human family. The new frontier is that of *developmental accountability.* In our church programs and policies we must develop new ways of fighting the war against poverty in all its forms at home and abroad. If we have now accepted the emergence of the Third World as a reality in the South, we need to sit up and take notice that the Fourth World has already arrived on our own front lawns in the North, where excessive wealth and uncontrolled progress is an uncomfortable neighbor of homelessness, destitution, despair and mindless violence. In the Fourth World, under-developed peoples are no longer "over there"; they are, in fact, "right here."

Our final frontier is that of our *ecological responsibility.* The word *human* means to be of the soil, the earth, the ground. Human beings are earthy people, and the earth to which we belong and to which we return is truly our mother and not our slave. The contemporary experiences of the pollution on land, across the oceans and in the atmosphere we share, are pitiful testimony to our growing irresponsibility. To be made in the image of God does not merely imply the dignity we should expect as persons, it also points to the responsibility which is ours to care for God's creation in the way which God cares for it. Concern for the human and material ecology is an inherent part of our Christian responsibility, and we need to explore new ways of keeping this ministry alive. Whether we are atheists, Muslims or Christians, there is only one earth for all of us. Our churches have not been vocal enough about their ecological tasks and responsibilities. We must really mean it when we say with the psalmist: "O Lord, how manifold are thy works, in wisdom hast thou made them all: the earth is full of thy riches" (Ps 104:24).

It may well be that the fifteen frontiers which I have just outlined simply reflect the errant mind of one who knows little about the hard facts of life. It may also be that the dominant ecclesiology that has come through in these suggestions bears little resemblance to the church with which many others might be familiar. For many, the church is nothing more than a function of the society as a whole, a microcosm as it were. For some, the church is the last bastion of our most private feelings and innermost hopes, the guardian of the values we cherish, beyond the reach of clumsy hands or irreverent schemes. Such estimates are legitimate, but they may not necessarily flow from the gospel of Jesus Christ whose Spirit unifies, socializes, transforms and sanctifies the community of believers.

The new frontiers suggested here are the result of a prolonged process of reflection on four basic theological propositions. *One*, the church is a community of charisms, or gifts, derived from the Spirit of Christ, and freely given for our witness in the world. *Two*, the distinctions we make between progressives and conservatives are antithetical to the call of God to the church to be the church. *Three*, we need to get back to the more frequent study and use of the Bible, so that we might discover new dimensions of the divine imperative, God's constant call to us to do mission and ministry. *Four*, the church must live as an anticipatory community, breaking new ground in becoming, in the here and the now, what we understand God's heaven to be all about.

If we truly believe that in Christ we are a new creation, then at the very least we ourselves owe it to posterity to make the effort to become the new creation, rather than to merely find ways of talking about it. This involves a readiness to see ourselves as ministers of Christ, set apart by God for a distinctive work and witness in God's world. What are some of the theological implications that flow from such a self-understanding, especially in the light of these new frontiers? It is to be hoped that the discussion in the chapters that follow will add some useful insights for further reflection on these vital questions in the life of our churches today.

CHAPTER THREE

CHRISTIAN
MINISTRY AND
THE WAY

W HAT HAPPENS TO ATHEISTS WHEN THEY DIE? THIS
is one of the many opening questions I
have often posed to students in my
classes in systematic theology at the
Howard University School of Divinity. Other questions
deal with such topics as prayer. What really happens
when we pray? Are we just talking to ourselves? Or suppose there is no God—then what happens to persons of
faith? I have always received a wide array of answers to
the question about atheists. Each answer has always
tended to reflect not only a personal acquaintance with
the mind of God, or the plan of God, or the justice of God,
or the word of God (in the Bible), but also a strong sense
of the possession of a monopoly on heaven held by
Christians, and only by some Christians at that! Heaven is
reserved for Christians only, they seem to say.

The question has always intrigued me. Not because I
believe that anyone has the answer but mainly because it
can trigger a barrage of responses from highly motivated
people who are sincere in their beliefs, eloquent in their

convictions, and adamant in their religious determinations. They firmly believe that they know the mind of God, for they found it in the Bible, God's Book.

It is not difficult to imagine the variety of answers that such a question about atheists evokes. Some are convinced that they will go straight to hell, because they have not known Jesus Christ as Lord and Savior, or have not been saved, washed and sanctified. Some are convinced that atheists are not really atheists, that there can really be no such person. God would never allow it, they think. People who call themselves atheists, they say, have some sort of god whom they worship, even if they do not know its name.

Others might respond that this is really a nonanswer, because there must be some resolution of the problem of belief and nonbelief. If people claim to be atheists, they say, then we just have to take their word for it. Some make so bold as to allow that there might be some intermediate stage between death and the final disposition of souls, even if they shy away from calling that stage purgatory. Few are quick to say that they really do not know; still fewer are ready to allow the love of God to work in surprising ways, such as atheists being received into heaven's gates because they too are God's creatures.

I tend to leave the question as a question, without attempting to arrive at any consensus or resolution. There are two important reasons for this. First, it leaves open the fact that qualifications for heaven or hell are not determined by persons other than the God who is Lord of heaven and earth, however much we may consider ourselves competent to decide on God's behalf. Second, the claim which Jesus makes about himself—that he is the way, the truth and the life, and that no one comes to the Father but through him (Jn 14:6)—gets in the way of so much of the theological debate about the mystery of God's forgiving and saving grace that we need to expose the danger of its misuse as early as possible.

There are, of course, convincing arguments in favor of heavenly rewards for earthly efforts. There are also convincing arguments in favor of atheists not wanting to get to heaven, since they did not believe in the existence of such a place when they could have. But we must be careful not to restrict ourselves merely to what we expect to find in heaven if we ever get there. There is a popular song which says: *"When we all get to heaven, / What a day of rejoicing that will be; / When we all see Jesus, / We'll sing and shout the victory."* We should not be that quick to rule out a share in that victory for atheism as we know it, even if we think that such a sad (or bad!) human condition needs to be abandoned, rather than be made victorious. Heavenly rejoicing will be triggered by many startling surprises about who and what we will find there, simply because God's ways and God's thoughts are radically different from our ways and our thoughts. The beatific vision is not within our province to define or control. Thank God for that!

Thus, if Jesus is truly to be the way, the truth, and the life, what does this say to us about life on earth? How does this generate for people of faith the necessary ingredients for faithful obedience and witness to the call of God in Christ? Or does the concern for getting a passport into heaven take precedence over the concern for the way we live out our life on earth? Religious zeal often seems to overflow into areas of concern that are beyond our competence to articulate, but never beyond our need to speculate. We must always be careful to recognize that the way to heaven for us does not consist in taking the beltway around the realities of earth, with all its grounds for belief and unbelief, with all the glimmers of hope and torrents of despair. The seeds of atheism are generated as much from within the community of belief as they are generated from without.

When I was a seminarian at Codrington College, Barbados, in the 1960s, there was a gardener there whose name was Wiltshire. Wiltshire would never miss an opportunity to engage the seminarians in some sort of religious discussion, for this helped him in two ways. It gave him an opportunity to test his knowledge, opinions and beliefs against those of the students. It also gave him an excuse to rest from his labors in the sun-drenched gardens of the campus. Wiltshire had one stock answer to the question about how many people were going to heaven. He always claimed that he did not know what the final count would be, but that he was sure that 144,000 had already reached there. His authority for such statistical data was based on information available to him from the last book in the Bible. Wiltshire's concern was about quantity rather than quality. My students at Howard are much more concerned about the latter, and they also claim biblical authority for their position.

Yet this is not what really makes sense for the task of the Christian at this time. This is not what brings the Christian into full confrontation, and active conversation, with the trials and tribulations of modern living. It does not help very much in our keeping faith in a world where faith is sometimes of little apparent worth, or of trying to be "good" when all the "bad" people are getting by so well. In an age and culture that is driven almost entirely by the efficacy of the bottomline and by the insatiable need to reap the tangible fruits of profitable living, where greed and excess are inseparable cousins, Christians are constantly being challenged to live out their convictions under the pale of material deficits. Is there a guaranteed way to respond to such a challenge?

It used to be said that while theologians argued furiously about how many angels danced on the head of a pin, the world was sinking fast in sin. We need to be careful that such scenarios no longer occur within the religious and theological community. The critical issue for us as people of faith is how to hold fast to that which is both good and godly, in a cultural context of massive countervailing circumstances and major contradictions. What does it take to be a faithful Christian in the modern world? Who helps us in our determination to follow Jesus as the way, the truth and the life?

It is logical for us to assume that the claim about Jesus as the way, the truth and the life is meant for us as faithful followers. It is not meant to be the exclusionary clause for non-Christians and atheists. Indeed, when the Risen Christ was questioned about another disciple (the disciple whom Jesus loved), about whom Simon Peter seemed to be quite concerned, Jesus simply urged him to mind his own business (Jn 21:22). "What does it matter to you if I want him to hold on till I come back?" Jesus asked, "just follow me." This is both a rebuke and advice for all those who might wish to pontificate on the qualifications for heaven for persons other than themselves. We should be chiefly concerned with what it means to live out the Christian life, to share and share in the faith of Jesus, and to join in loyal fellowship with all those who work for the breaking in of the Realm of God into our human history. In all this some atheists may well be our allies. We are often warned about wolves in sheep's clothing, but seldom do we remember that there are also sheep in wolves' clothing. God always knows the difference but we often do not. Professing atheists may well be active angels unaware.

As faithful Christians, we are assured that Jesus is the only way to God. But we are not to assume that there are no other paths available to those whom God calls to Godself in many and various other ways. This is precisely why we should pay particular attention to the meaning of the gospel as the Way, the Word and the Truth. There are special implications for us who seek to do ministry, to evangelize, and also seek the unity of the faith in the bond of peace and justice. What is the Way to which the gospel of Jesus points the followers of Jesus? What is the Word to be proclaimed, and how must that be heard and acted upon? What is the Truth that Christians hold in common? What happens to it when we handle it with our clumsy hands behind our dividing lines? The rest of this chapter will focus on the ministry of the Way. We will examine how the Way is inextricably bound up with the ministry of Truth and the power of the Word in the service of God through Christ. This is in sharp distinction from a ministry of powerful words from people in power.

The Ministry of The Way

It is critically important for us to recall that one of the earliest names for the new religion of Jesus was "The Way." It seems to have been even earlier than the term "Christianity." Saul of Tarsus had received a mandate from the high priest to go to the synagogues in Damascus to weed out any who were followers of The Way (Acts 9:2). He was to bring them bound to Jerusalem. Paul himself later refers to his new religion as "The Way" on several occasions. For example, he gives this testimony about his faith: This I admit to you, that according to the Way, which they call a sect, I worship the God of our ancestors, believing everything laid down according to the law or written in the prophets. (Acts 24:14). In the Acts of the Apostles we are also introduced to the African Christian, Apollos, an eloquent, theologically educated, enthusiastic follower of Jesus who had been "instructed in the Way of the Lord" (Acts 18:25). He is taken in by Priscilla and Aquila and is given a more accurate explanation of the

"Way of God." It is possible to assume that Priscilla's "Way of God" catechism was far more comprehensive than Apollos' "Way of the Lord" experience. But it would be difficult to suggest that Apollos was any less committed to following Jesus as The Way before he met this exuberant missionary couple.

The symbol of The Way obviously had a very important impact on the minds of the earliest Christians, for it commanded a radically new challenge of faith in terms of discipleship and witness. It had nothing to do with "method," or "custom" or "habit." It had to do with new life. The Way was the new life of the Risen Christ experienced through the Spirit of God. The new religion was the way of salvation, or the way of peace, or the way of the Lord or the way of God. It was the path for the pilgrimage of faith. It was the context in which the meaning of Jesus was to become lived out in their freshly corporate life. The new Christians were sharers in the way of faith. This was constantly held out to them as being critical for a life of loving fellowship and radical hope for the future, in spite of their difficulties and struggles. So it was Christ who had opened up to them the "new and living way" (Heb 10:20) to God. Thus, the *way of Jesus was the way to Jesus, and the way to Jesus was the way to God.* He who once proclaimed the way to God now himself becomes the way to God.

This concept of The Way was itself deeply rooted in the spirituality of the ancient people of God. The Way of the Lord was bound up with the Law of the Lord. Particularly in the Psalms, we often encounter people of the Covenant calling on God to teach them the way, to show them the way. God's word was for them like a lantern to their feet, a light to their path. The Way of the Lord was the way of righteousness, which led to salvation and deliverance. The way of the ungodly led to perdition.

Modern theologians still give special attention to the

symbol of the way as a paradigm of response to the call of God to faith, or even as a means of understanding the mystery of God in Jesus as the Christ. For example, the German theologian Jurgen Moltmann, in his recent study on Christology, *The Way Of Jesus Christ*, explains why he found the symbol of the way to be a most appropriate and convenient concept for his theological discussion. He offers three reasons for this. First, he says that the symbol of the way "embodies the aspect of process, and brings out christology's alignment toward its goal." Second, the symbol of the way "makes us aware that every human christology is historically conditioned and limited." In this regard, Moltmann speaks of every Christology as a Christology on the way, and not yet a "christology of the home country." It is one of faith, not one of sight. Third, he says that "every way is an invitation," something which we are to follow. He continues: "Anyone who enters upon Christ's way will discover who Jesus really is; and anyone who really believes in Jesus as the Christ of God will follow him along the way he himself took."[20] It is the determination to do ministry as a follower of Jesus that will mainly occupy our attention for the rest of this chapter.

I have already referred to some of my students and their varying responses to the possible fate of atheists in the afterlife. I now wish to refer to another group of students at the Howard University School of Divinity with whom I have had some very stimulating, engaging, exciting and helpful debates. In a seminar for doctoral students we bring together our insights about the nature of the Christian ministry and the many challenges such a vocation brings with it. The group is mostly comprised of students who are already in the ordained ministry, and who bring with them a wealth of experience both as ministers and as professionals in their own right. Yet it is important to point out that the issues about ministry *are not confined to the ordained ministry.*

Some of these students are founders of their own congregations, while some are exploring new visions for ministry. Some hold very responsible positions in their denominations. Some are chaplains of institutions—educational, medical, military. Some are public servants or federal government officers, some are teachers. All are blessed with wide and enriching backgrounds. They seek to bring with them their past experiences and their spiritual pilgrimages, and to distill the benefits of such gifts within the context of a collective search for fresh ways of understanding their vocation to ministry. Many of them are spouses and parents who have to interpret their programs of study in such a way that would involve the commitment and support of their families as they wrestle with the many just demands on their time, energy and interests. In short, there are pressures within and pressures without. Challenges abound and problems surround them. But so do tremendous possibilities for witness and service. Thus they seek new ways of understanding what it takes to be both a committed Christian and a dedicated Christian minister, for one cannot be understood apart from the other. How can they follow the ways of ministry and also point others to The Way of Jesus through their ministry? This is their fervent quest.

As we have wrestled together in the seminars, trying to discern the fundamental characteristics of a Christian minister, we have searched for the most appropriate attributes and virtues that are constitutive of such a life of faith, witness and service. We have come up with a wide variety of answers, all of which carry some degree of merit and which, when taken together, provide a cumulative profile—one which is too comprehensive for any single person to fit. We have suggested such characteristics as commitment, dedication, loyalty, honesty, integrity, compassion, faith in God, perseverance, humor, courage, patience, boldness, obedience, discipline, trustworthiness, flexibility, self-awareness, open-mindedness, vision, vocation, humility, listening to God. There has been a general consensus that the minister should always be a person of untiring service for God's people, while at the same time being a faithful witness to the life of salvation. We have found ourselves in general agreement that the minister's role should include being an encourager of the faithful, with the capacity to empower others to bear faithful witness. Such a capacity should always find its source in the Spirit of God.

A careful analysis of the responses to our basic question has provided us with the following five characteristics, on which we have found general agreement: *compassion, commitment, courage, integrity, and discipline.* Each characteristic requires some discussion here, as we seek to understand what this ministry of The Way ought to entail.

Compassion on The Way

There can be little doubt that the virtue of *compassion* enjoys pride of place in any serious assessment of the public ministry of Jesus of Nazareth. Not only does Jesus speak of the compassion which he himself feels for those whom he encounters, but he also places great emphasis on compassion as a characteristic of the principal figures in many of his parable stories. Preeminently, however, his supreme act of faithful obedience to the God whom he calls Father, namely, his sacrificial death on the cross, becomes for people of faith the paradigm of compassion in the history of the human family. So the Jesus who feels compassion for the hungering multitudes, and feeds them miraculously with five loaves and a few fish, is the Jesus who also weeps like a child at the grave of Lazarus his friend. He is the one who readily identifies with Bartimaeus, a blind and uppity beggar. He deals graciously with a persistent Syrophoenician woman. Mary Magdalene, a woman thought by some to be of questionable virtue, becomes his first witness of the Easter miracle. None of these persons was highly thought of by their contemporaries.

The Gospel leaves us in no doubt whatsoever that Jesus has shown us what it means to flesh out the meaning of compassion. The Jesus of the gospel is truly the "man for others." He demonstrates throughout his ministry the importance of taking seriously the poor, the marginalized, the suffering, the hopeless, the homeless, the broken, the unlettered and the despised. In other words, the way of compassion is not simply a device for dealing with the pain of the world, it is more significantly the way of salvation for the world. Compassion means suffering with others, entering unconditionally into their pain and brokenness, bearing with them the agonies of meaninglessness and despair, of loss and the threat of death, knowing that beyond such a condition there is the promise of new life.

It would be highly presumptuous to seek to define precisely what compassion is. We do better to confine ourselves to seeking an understanding of what compassion does. We do better by trying to understand what Jesus meant by what he did, and by attempting to make it come alive in ways which are suggested by the cultural and historical contexts of our day. It is sufficient to say what compassion is not. We need not be unduly exercised in trying to arrive at a definition for it. We are expected to live it out, not spell it out. Every age has its own way of pointing to its own experience and expression of compassion. This is why the Christian ministry of The Way must become the primary focus for those who would take their call to ministry seriously. They must see in it not a convenient option for the fainthearted, but the basic task of those who are called to follow Jesus as the Way of compassion.

Compassion requires strength of will, consistency of vision, sensitivity of heart and firmness of spirit. Our Christian habits must include a fresh and daily outpouring of Christlike compassion, especially for those who are broken and torn by the vulnerabilities of life, or by the harsh realities of injustice in our societies. We rob ourselves of a great deal of our own humanity when we wait for crises to erupt before we reach out to people in Christlike compassion. Compassion is truly like an ongoing heavenly symphony on earth; it requires constant practice and daily rehearsals.

Perhaps the greatest African-American mystic of the twentieth century has been Howard Thurman. He is certainly one of the most profound Christian thinkers of our time. Thurman spoke of compassion in terms of "awareness." In one of his most moving passages on this theme, he had this to say:

> God is making room in my heart for compassion: the
> awareness that where my life begins is where your life
> begins; the awareness that the sensitiveness to your
> needs cannot be separated from the sensitiveness to
> my needs; the awareness that the joys of my heart are
> never mine alone—nor are my sorrows.[21]

One of the most disappointing aspects of life in the 1980s in the United States was the fact that while some fortunate people were counting their economic blessings under the Reagan administration, saying to themselves that they had never had it so good, countless others had exactly the opposite experience. They had never had it so bad. Life became harder for them. Their social conditions worsened. Their access to civic benefits and employment opportunities were diminished. In the end, it was said of this President of the richest country in the world that during his presidency he managed to make the denial of compassion respectable again. A new phrase was added to the common public discourse—"compassion fatigue."

For the Christian minister today, therefore, Christian compassion is the way through which the meaning of Jesus will best be proclaimed, and the efficacy of divine grace will best become fleshed out. It is the urgent task of the Christian minister today to make the reality of compassion contagious again, thereby counteracting the ripple effects of the denial of compassion during the last decade. Such a reversal of experience should not be left to the political directorate at any level of our national life. We now know that phrases such as "kinder and gentler nation" do not bring about a reversal of fortunes for the dispossessed and the broken among us. We also know that various brands of religious conservatism do not bring it about either.

To minister in the Way of Compassion must never be taken as a soft option on the part of those who would seek to follow Jesus as The Way. To minister in the Way of Compassion must never be understood as the form of least resistance to the harsh realities of life, especially where such realities produce pain, suffering and uncomfortable relationships. To minister in the Way of Compassion should not be regarded as the means of religious escape from the practical implications of living in a world of cruel vice and unrelenting sin. To minister in the Way of Compassion is to seek to live unconditionally in that very Way, through the patient practice of compassion among those who would be tempted to take each other for granted, or to be overcome by strong feelings of contempt or vicious resentment. For just as divine compassion is supremely expressed in the fact that Jesus, as the Lamb of God, both takes on and takes away the sin of the world, so too must our faithful response to such compassion demonstrate our solidarity with the human condition, as well as our commitment to its reconciliation and liberation.

Commitment to The Way

Our doctoral students also said that *commitment* is an essential characteristic in the life and witness of the Christian minister. Here again, the example of Jesus in the gospel becomes pivotal for our understanding of what this virtue of commitment is all about. Jesus continually reminds his followers that there can be no ambivalence or double-mindedness about Christian discipleship. He speaks of the Christian life as walking on the straight and narrow pathway. He speaks of the importance of not turning back, after we have put our hands to the plow. To look back, he says, is to render ourselves unfit for the Realm of God. He speaks of the impossibility of serving two masters at the same time. In an often-misunderstood remark about the Realm, Jesus gives praise to those who have made themselves eunuchs for the sake of the Realm of God.

Above all, he expresses the true meaning of Christian commitment in his summary of the Law—love of God with heart, mind, soul, and strength, and one's neighbor as oneself. Yet nothing that Jesus says about the meaning of commitment can supersede what he actually does throughout his whole life and ministry. His life of total, complete and unconditional filial obedience to God, which culminates on the cross, gives us the supreme example of what we are to understand by Christian commitment. Thus, his last words from the cross—"Father, into your hands I commend my spirit"—are not just about his dying but rather about the totality of his life. Jesus lived his life wholly toward God, whom he called Father.

To follow Jesus as The Way truly involves the Christian minister in the life of total commitment. Various sectors of our common life demand commitment of its constituencies—families, fraternities, sororities, corporations, political organizations, marriages, social movements—even underground movements. Commitment is not simply the fundamental condition through which effective ministry may be exercised. More importantly, it is the means whereby the true meaning of what ministers seek to bear witness to in their lives, or to demonstrate in their personal conduct, becomes available to others who are searching for moral and spiritual leadership, personal assurance, emotional encouragement and religious authenticity. The "do-as-I-say-but-not-as-I-do" syndrome, so common among us as a temptation, must always be regarded as inimical to the high calling to Christian ministry.

Howard Thurman understands commitment in terms of surrender. He suggests that such commitment means the surrender of all that we are and have. It involves the nerve centers of our consent, the outlying districts of ourselves, the things in our world to which we are related, our hopes, dreams, and desires. He speaks of self-surrender as the central factor in our communion with God. Thurman thus urges our hearts with these words:

> I surrender myself to God without any conditions or reservations. I shall not bargain with Him. I shall not make my surrender piecemeal but I shall lay bare the very center of me, that all of my very being shall be charged with the creative energy of God. Little by little, or vast area by vast area, my life must be transmuted in the life of God. As this happens, I come into

> the meaning of true freedom and the burdens that I
> seemed unable to bear are floated in the current of
> the life and love of God.[22]

The life of commitment involves much more than the love of correctness, whether theological, liturgical, symbolical, political, ideological or social. The significance of creating a personal harmony between the external appearance and the inner intention is always of critical value for those who would attempt to serve God's people in God's name. Creating impressions in the ministry for the sake of popularity is just as pharisaical as the hypocrisy which Jesus so roundly condemned in his day. Modern-day pharisaism is just as antithetical to a life of genuine Christian commitment as is racism to the ethos of modern decency.

There can be no real commitment without some form of conversion. For conversion to be a lifelong experience, there has to be the experience of community. In other words, commitment, conversion and community go together. This is the crux of the life of commitment—the member of the community is a member precisely because there has been some form of incorporation into that community, as well as some definite commitment to promote and uphold what that community stands for. Conversion is not a once-and-for-all act. It is a daily, lifelong inescapable mode of living out all that the community would wish to generate and sustain through its total membership. In Christian terms, the life of commitment is synonymous with the life in the Spirit, and it is only through that shared life in the Spirit that the effects of community, as well as its benefits, can be mediated both to its membership and beyond.

The life of commitment is one of radical persistence— the life which knows how to keep on keeping on. Eugene

Peterson says this very well: "The mark of a certain kind of genius is the ability and energy to keep returning to the same task relentlessly, imaginatively, curiously, for a lifetime. Never give up and go on to something else; never get distracted and be diverted to something else."[23] Such sentiments may come up against the human thirst for variety and adventure, the thrill of new ways of life, the boredom of routine and the mechanistic drudgery of the familiar. But the test of true commitment must surely be in the maturity of being held accountable for that which is one's duty and responsibility, regardless of the difficulties involved.

After all, there is in human experience much that would urge us to get a move on. We constantly get the itch to look for greener pastures, or at least to shift our station in life. This is a common tendency among ordained ministers when conditions in the pastorate no longer meet their expectations. It is true that one finds it virtually impossible to sustain any sense of commitment to that which seems to be derelict, counterproductive or even risky. Nevertheless, there is a quality in human life which requires that we hold fast to a sense of that which is good, even when there is a cost involved. Michael Downey puts it this way: "Our commitments are ways of making good on life. They are ways of expressing, of naming what and whom we live for."[24]

The sociological studies of R. M. Kanter provide us with a scientific understanding of the ways in which human beings demonstrate commitment to groups and institutions. Kanter suggests that there are at least six commitment mechanisms that can be observed, particularly in groups. She lists these as: Sacrifice, Investment, Renunciation, Communion, Mortification, and Transcendence.[25] It is interesting to note that Kanter's notion of transcendence seems to be the equivalent of what Thurman calls "surrender." While these appear to be indicative of an institutional or communal commitment, it seems to me that something more is required of Christian commitment. To quote Downey again: "Christian commitment requires risking security and stability so that his (Christ's) way is the only way in which we place our trust."[26]

The Christian minister, then, is called to a life of commitment that involves four indispensable factors. The first is *self-denial*. This comes directly from the invitation of Jesus to those who would follow him. He says that they must deny themselves and take up their cross daily and follow him. Commitment in the ministry requires a life of constant self-denial. This is not to say that we are called upon to deny who we are, but rather that we are called upon to ensure that no claims which we make about ourselves, or on ourselves, should ever take precedence over the claims which God makes on us and our lives in Christ.

The second factor is that of *self-sacrifice*. The fact that the minister is called by God to a life of constant devotion and sacrifice means that there will always be a challenge to offer up tirelessly all that is valuable and precious in the life of that minister. Sacrifice means offering up to God that which is of true and lasting value. The offering up of one's self—our souls and our bodies—makes the life of self-sacrifice not only meaningful but also exemplary. For the minister is one who both serves and leads, and neither is possible, nor effective, without a life of genuine and compelling example.

The third factor is that of *self-consecration*. This has to do with the life of holiness, that setting apart of one's entire being for the total and unconditional disposal of the divine will. Self-consecration calls for the devotion of one's priorities and values toward the greater bringing in of the victory of love and forgiveness—the conquest of life and salvation over the forces of sin, evil, hatred and human meanness. The consecrated life thus does not become the life of escape and withdrawal, but rather the life of radical engagement in a world that offers so many alternatives to the call of God in Jesus Christ. In popular parlance, it calls on the minister to work out in existential ways what is meant by living *in the world* without being *of the world.*

The fourth factor is that of *solidarity.* The life of commitment always creates in the mind of the Christian the need for an honest answer to the question, commitment to what? But even as we seek to revisit what we are to be committed to as Christians, we dare not forget that we are not alone in this life of Christian commitment. The faith that we share in Christ we share in common with others. This means that commitment and solidarity with persons of faith are of inseparable worth and importance.

These four factors then, self-denial, self-sacrifice, self-consecration, and solidarity are essential ingredients of the life of commitment for the minister. Who is sufficient for these things? It requires the virtue of courage as a direct gift from God to God's people of faith. We now turn to the virtue of courage, which is the third major characteristic in the life of the Christian minister.

Courage for The Way

Although it is known as one of the four cardinal virtues (along with prudence, justice, and temperance), the word *courage* (in the Greek, *andreia*) does not show up anywhere in the New Testament. The Acts of the Apostles (28:15) uses the word *tharsos,* which suggests more of the sense of cheerfulness than of fortitude. Even the word for boldness (*parrhesia*) has more to do with freedom and confidence of speech than with strength of character. Unless it can be convincingly demonstrated that the apostolic church considered that the emphasis of the three

Christian virtues of faith, hope, and love far outweighed the importance of the four cardinal virtues, we are left to wonder how much weight the virtue of courage carried in that era of the church's witness. No one can deny that the courage of martyrdom, and the Christians' determination to bear witness to the risen Christ and the gospel in the face of gravely overwhelming conditions was courage *par excellence*. Yet it is striking to note that the apostolic proclamation was able to effectively create a new grammar for spirituality and evangelism without much use of the word *courage* itself. What then do we say about courage as a virtue inherent in the ministerial character?

No ethical system can get very far without an emphasis on courage. The Greek philosopher Plato regarded it as an important virtue to be mastered by the Guardians of the City (in his *Republic*), especially as they had to be able to distinguish between things which they ought to fear and those which they ought not. Aristotle went further and made a clear distinction between real courage and some spurious forms, such as the courage that arose mainly from anger or other emotions, or that which evolved from respect for another person's authority or opinion. In some respects, it may well be said that Aristotle helped to lay the groundwork for the proper distinction between moral courage and physical courage. We are principally concerned with moral courage, although the teachings of such early divines as Ambrose of Milan and Augustine of Hippo tended to place a combined emphasis on both moral and physical courage as a necessary condition for withstanding sin's temptation and the threat of martyrdom.

In a sermon which he delivered at Harvard on St. Bartholomew's Day (August 24, 1848) entitled "Work And Play," the famous Congregationalist preacher Horace Bushnell offered a very sharp distinction between "courage" and "bravery." On the one hand, courage was "the greatness of a great heart; the repose and confidence of a man whose soul is rested in truth and principle."[27] On the other hand, he said that "bravery is of the will.... Enter the heart and you shall find, too often, a dastard spirit lurking in your hero. Call him still a brave man, if you will, only remember that he lacks courage."[28] He spoke of bravery as a "very imposing and plausible counterfeit." Faith, he said, was the nerve of courage, while risk was the plague and tremor of bravery. In a very telling commentary on his day, Bushnell offered this homiletical sentiment:

> In the infatuated zeal of our race for the acquisition of money, in war, in chivalry, in perverted religion— in all these forms, covering almost the whole ground of humanity with counterfeits of play, that are themselves the deepest movements of the race, I show you the boundless sweep of this divine instinct, [religion] and how surely we may know that the perfected state of man is a state of beauty, truth, and love, where life is its own end and joy.[29]

We need to distinguish human bravery, or even rashness, from Christian courage. Without such a distinction we are liable to equate every act of resistance to fear as having religious or spiritual significance. This is clearly not what is to be understood by that important New Testament word *parrhesia* (boldness) as the dominant quality of the apostolic church. The Jewish authorities recognize the boldness of Peter and John, in the face of their warnings, and call to mind that they had been associated with the crucified Jesus of Nazareth (Acts 4:13). The word *boldness* appears on two other occasions in that same chapter. Through faith in Christ we have boldness and confidence to approach God (Eph 3:12). The writer of the Letter to the Hebrews urges us to use our *boldness* by which we have entered into a new and living way, opened for us through the blood of Christ, as the basis for our perseverance and constancy of faith and public witness. It is that same virtue by which we are to provoke one another as Christians to love and good works, *not neglecting to meet together, as is the habit of some, but encouraging one another* (10:25).

Christian courage as "boldness," then, is not merely for personal empowerment or individualistic gratification. It is a gift of God's Spirit to be used for, and on the behalf of, the community of faith for the strengthening of the witness and the deepening of the hope that we share in Christ. We are brought to a stark realization that the Christian way always involves the reality of fear. It is a fearful thing to be a Christian in the modern world. And yet, the New Testament gives the antidote to fear in terms of love rather than in terms of courage. The First Letter of John places the emphasis on the love of God, freely made available to us first, by God's abiding in us, as that by which we can overcome fear. *Love has been perfected among us in this: that we may have boldness* [parrhesia] *on the day of judgment, because as he is, so are we in this world. There is no fear in love, but perfect love casts out fear; for fear has to do with punishment, and whoever fears has not reached perfection in love (4:17,18).*

Divine love and Christian courage therefore go together. Courage, as one of the main instruments for the Christian Way, stands at the very heart of what it takes to function as a servant of the gospel. One writer makes this very helpful assertion: "Christians learn that courage is a necessity rather than a virtue through their frequent meditation on the passion and triumph of our Lord. In every generation orthodox doctrine and individual piety are most clearly expressed in the compassion and courage of church members. Where there is no courage, compassion dwindles and where compassion is absent courage tends to become arrogant self-display."[30] The words of President Nelson Mandela of South Africa are also very instructive here: "I learned that courage was not the absence of fear, but the triumph over it. I felt fear myself more times than I can remember, but I hid it behind a mask of boldness. The brave man is not he who does not feel afraid, but he who conquers that fear."[31] We shall have more to learn from Mandela in our closing chapters. Suffice it to say for now that the meaning of courage has hardly come alive in our contemporary experience in a nobler way than in the successful struggle for liberation and freedom which he has so richly embodied in his total being and personal story.

Integrity of The Way

Integrity is perhaps one of the most abused words in our common discourse these days. Why is this so? It seems to me that the word has become saddled with all sorts and conditions of meaning, especially by those who would rush to claim authenticity or correctness, structural power, or an image of moral superiority. The word finds itself into the language of defense for any number of different causes. We often hear of "Integrity Commissions," bodies of persons being appointed to examine charges of impropriety, or a lack of integrity, on the part of public persons. So in the final analysis, the word integrity is often associated with the search for the truth, or the pursuit of truth, or the expression of truth. We speak of the integrity of systems, structures, and fabrics as well as the integrity of persons, and somehow we are attempting to associate that which is genuine with that which is durable.

What is important to remember in all this, however, is that "integrity" as a word takes its meaning from the Latin word for "freshness." Integrity is first and foremost an experience, as well as an expression of that which is fresh and radiant, that which is bright and renewing, that which is both rich and enriching. The Integrity of The Way, therefore, takes its cue from the impact which the person and ministry of Jesus of Nazareth made on the persons whom he encountered. They recognized that, in this plain and unheralded outsider from Nazareth, something genuine had come from God that they had never experienced before, and that they were hardly likely to experience again. Could this be the Messiah? This was the question from the woman at the well of Samaria. There was something quite distinctive about him and his conversation. Could anything good come out of Nazareth? This was Nathaniel's question to Philip. Philip could only advise him to come and see for himself. Nathaniel's eventual acceptance of Jesus was clearly a recognition of messianic integrity.

This unmistakable soundness of character, freshness of presence, and clarity of message, produced in the hearers of Jesus that challenge of conviction and invitation of response which started the whole movement we call Christianity. This is what we must now understand and embrace as the "integrity" of The Way. It demands uprightness and perseverance, just as much as it requires wisdom and personal honesty, together with faith and spirit.

In his very helpful book *The Pastor as Evangelist* (1984), Professor Richard Stoll Armstrong wrote extensively about the importance of integrity in the personal life of the pastor, especially of the pastor's faith. He noted that personal faith was not only a matter of power, and a matter of example, but also a matter of integrity. He went on to give something of his own personal testimony. He wrote:

> As a pastor-evangelist I wanted to be able to make a
> rational case for an experiential faith, so that I could

preach, teach, evangelize, and bear witness with intellectual as well as spiritual integrity. The soul-searching process continues, but I now can say, after much reading, discussion, reflection, and prayer, that I know what I believe and why I believe it. That does not mean that I have all the answers to my faith questions. It means that I know what the questions are and which ones I can or cannot answer. I am aware of the limitations and the risks of faith, as well as of its possibilities and rewards. (p. 68)[32]

In furthering his insights on this important matter of integrity of faith, Armstrong also wrote the following: "The evangelist or witness must recognize the difference between the *what* and the *why* of faith. The objective of telling the *what* is to be understood; the objective of answering the *why* is to be believable. The *what* should give clarity to the *why*; the *why* should give integrity to the *what*" (pp. 68–9).

With Armstrong we affirm the importance of integrity in every aspect of the Christian life and witness. We affirm the importance of spiritual as well as intellectual integrity. We renounce the tendency to be manipulative, hypocritical or compromising in our confession of Jesus Christ as Lord and Savior, and in our active and public demonstration of what we are called to become for the sake of the Realm of God. It is difficult to believe that any Spirit-filled witness can at the same time be devoid of Spirit-led integrity.

Discipline through The Way

It is not very difficult to recognize that there is a close connection between the word *Discipline* and the word

Disciple. The latter is known to be one who is in the learning business, not just in the following business. Now, no learning takes place without a certain amount of discipline. The disciples of Jesus learned the discipline of following him, even when they did not fully understand who he was or what he was really about. It was in the course of time, most certainly after his departure from them, that they came to realize that he was indeed "the Lord." This was for them the true meaning of their resurrection experience. Thus it was that during the course of their discipleship they embraced the discipline of patiently waiting to understand more clearly what was unfolding before their eyes throughout the course of Jesus' earthly ministry. They followed Jesus as The Way during his ministry, and were therefore in a position to proclaim him as the Way to God through patient suffering, a daily waiting on God and a persistent determination to proclaim the gospel to the ends of the earth.

Discipline for us can mean no less. It points us to the basic requirements for a ready openness to God's ongoing and surprising self-disclosures. It points us to the fundamental nature of the life of the Christian minister who seeks to understand not only what is the word of the Lord, but also how that word is to be interpreted and proclaimed with boldness and clarity. It points us to the need for constant prayer, careful and diligent study, quiet meditation and purposeful interaction with persons of faith or no faith. It calls for the sober sharing of ourselves, a steady wrestling with the issues of faith, and a willingness to point others to the meaning of hope and renewal of faith in their own lives. Above all, it points us to the need to live faithfully as witnesses to Christ in a world which would really prefer that there were no Christ to contend with.

Earlier in this chapter I referred to my earlier days as a seminarian at Codrington College in Barbados. We often had the opportunity to visit other islands of the Caribbean besides our island homes, especially during the long summer vacation. Of course, any kind of vacation from Codrington College was always welcome, since as students we lived under semi-monastic rules and regulations, with a fairly strict discipline of community life imposed by the college authorities, the Mirfield Fathers (Community of the Resurrection). It was during one such summer vacation that I visited the island of Trinidad for the first time (1963). Many encounters and experiences on that visit still linger in my mind. Yet chief among them were two encounters, both related to the matter of discipline.

The first encounter was with two students from Mauritius who were studying agriculture at the University of the West Indies, St. Augustine's Campus, at that time. Both students were Muslims. I well remember how enthusiastically they spoke about their own habits of religious discipline. They both affirmed that they found it impossible to spend their days comfortably unless they observed the five times for prayer every day. This struck me forcibly in my young and tender years as a theological student in training for the Anglican priesthood, for there was I making a great fuss about having to recite the daily offices (Morning Prayer and Evening Prayer) as a required rule of life. Their innocence and religious enthusiasm for their religious discipline put my own reluctance to shame.

The second encounter made things even worse for my young rebellious mind. I visited the barracks of the Trinidad Regiment one day, at a place called Chaguaramas. There I met several members of the military establishment. One of them, whose name I no longer remember, made a memorable assertion to me about himself in the course of our conversation. He said: "The only thing I like more than discipline is more discipline." Coming from a professional soldier this was quite understandable. But hearing it as a young seminarian who had to contend with a life of religious discipline was not easy to take. Both encounters have stayed with me, because they continue to teach me about the importance of learning the meaning and value of discipline through following Jesus as The Way. I also learned that true discipline really cannot be imposed; it has to come from within as a result of a daily meeting between ourselves and the God who is the source of our very being.

Much more than that, however, discipline through The Way involves suffering for the sake of Christ, for the sake of the truth, for the sake of the gospel and for the sake of human salvation. This is the high point of the message of the First Letter of Peter which, if we take it as an Easter pastoral sermon, combines the sharing in the resurrection of Christ with a sharing in the sufferings of Christ. He urges: *Prepare your minds for action; discipline yourselves; set all your hope on the grace that Jesus Christ will bring you when he is revealed* (1:13). Further, we are reminded that it is better to suffer for doing good than for doing evil. We should keep our consciences clear, *so that when you are maligned, those who abuse you for your good conduct in Christ may be put to shame* (3:16). To suffer as a Christian is a cause for pride and glory, it is not a disgrace (4:16). Such are the principles by which our ancestors in the faith learned the discipline of following Jesus as The Way.

For us there can be no compromise or negotiated amelioration. The follower of Christ must come to recognize that where there is the grace of God in the hearts of believers there is also strength to overcome the difficulties of true discipleship. Discipleship goes hand in hand with discernment, determination, devotion, and discipline. I am myself convinced that these five D's are more than sermon fodder. They are the means by which we feel within ourselves the sense of the nearness of God's presence in our lives, and the call to duty and discipline which is always inherent in the ministry of The Way.

●

In conclusion, we must come to recognize in Jesus that as the Way, the Truth, and the Life, we have an eternal call to faith and salvation, to repentance and reconciliation, to ministry and service to all of God's creatures, whether they are Christian or not. We follow in the steps of those who for two thousand years have called on his name, have confessed him as Lord and Savior of their lives, and have shared their faith with those in search of meaning and wholeness in their lives. For those who are called to ministry, there may be many characteristics to which they will be attracted, based principally on the context in which they find themselves. But, whatever the context, I remain convinced with my fellow students in the ministry that these five marks of ministry are as essential as they are divine, and that *compassion, courage, commitment, integrity,* and *discipline,* are more than mere characteristics. They are living and lively signs of God's abiding presence in the lives of those who are called to minister to God's people. For God always provides enough by which we might minister in God's name. The problem often is that we are not prepared to wait for it, as faithful servants of the Lord. Servants of God know that it is only by waiting on God that their strength can be renewed and sustained for the tasks that lie ahead. It is therefore to a discussion of ministry as servanthood that we will turn our attention in the next chapter.

CHAPTER FOUR

WHO SERVES
FIRST
SERVES BEST

THE PEOPLE OF HAITI HAVE SUFFERED MORE HARDSHIP AND turmoil than perhaps any other group of citizens in this hemisphere. Someone once wrote: "When Haitians look to the future, it is hard for them to imagine anything but continued bleakness."[33] Yet in spite of their persistent suffering they still maintain a hardiness of spirit, a strong commitment to living and an indomitable determination to survive. Haitians have often been treated as if they were "the wretched of the earth" in this region. One prominent Haitian cynically exclaimed: "The problem with the country of Haiti is that it is not a country."[34] Their claims to full humanity, or even to more civil compassion from their neighbors, have been consistently and systematically denied. But they have never lost heart. If at first they do not succeed, they try and try again. The following words of Jean-Bertrand Aristide (the former President of Haiti) bare the very soul of the Haitian people: "We are poor, it is true, but we have pride. We are poor, it is true, but we are courageous. We are poor, it is true, but we are people nonetheless. We know that the Lord created us in his image, and we the poor, who are abused, who are mistrusted, we are proud to be made in God's image. That pride will make us fight like the armies of God until the light of deliverance appears."[35] Why are the Haitians, poor as they are, so strong in cultural determination and common resolve? The answer lies in their deep religious traditions, their solidarity in suffering, and in their innate capacity to work and wait for the dawning of the New Day, regardless of the number of false starts and false messiahs.

What do the Haitians have to tell us about ministry, or discipleship, or service? Is it not true that their problem stems from all that Voodoo they practice at home? we ask self-righteously. Would they not be much better off if they could just put it away and follow in the blessed steps of their rich and righteous neighbors to the north? The fact is that the Haitians have much to teach others about the enduring qualities of the human spirit. They can teach us about the differences between materialistic servitude on the one hand, and creative servanthood in the midst of persistent poverty on the other. They can teach us about the social implications of the total synthesis of religion and life.

It seems to me that these lessons from the Haitian experience are of immediate relevance to our discussion in this chapter, as we seek to explore the meaning of Christian ministry in the process of becoming servants with Christ. For Christian discipleship as servanthood demands a strong endurance of the human spirit. It demands a clear determination of what being a servant is all about, a consciousness of whose servant we are. It allows for no disjuncture between faith and life. If Christian discipleship is the norm of life in the church as the community of faith, then servanthood is the essence of that discipleship. "If any one serves me, he must follow me; and where I am, there shall my servant be also; if any one serves me, the

Father will honor him" (Jn 12:26). These words of Jesus are quite precise and definitive, they allow for no wavering. But we must discuss the contemporary context in which such serving is inevitably undertaken.

The Context of Serving

The critical question for us as Christians today is a simple one: what does it mean to be a faithful follower of Jesus Christ in the postmodern world? How does one do this "Christian thing," become this Christian person, proclaim this Christian gospel by word and example? The question is simple, but the answer is complex. It is the duty of all Christians to seek and serve Christ in all persons, to strive for justice and peace among all people and to respect the dignity of every human being. But what does that really amount to when we are confronted with the pressures of daily living in a hostile, competitive and unfriendly environment?

The Episcopal Church's Catechism teaches that "the ministry of lay persons is to represent Christ and his Church; to bear witness to him wherever they may be; and, according to the gifts given them, to carry on Christ's work of reconciliation in the world; and to take their place in the life, worship, and governance of the Church" (*Book of Common Prayer,* p. 855). Yet such a job description hardly gets played out in full or taken very seriously by many. It is usually fast-forwarded to the easy part about worship and church governance. It is important for us to remind ourselves that entry into the ordained ministry does not signify a graduation out of the fundamental job description which the Catechism has assigned to all baptized persons.

To be a Christian in the postmodern world is to wrestle with the meaning of faith itself in a context of enormous countervailing pressures, both internally and externally. Internally, the person of faith is confronted with a number of very compelling forces. These can be listed as: Alienation, Anxiety, Absurdity, Apathy, Avarice, Agnosticism, Atheism. Let us call them the seven A's which threaten modern spiritual existence. A combination of these forces, in various configurations and levels of intensity, often forms the basic context in which persons wrestle with the work and witness of faith today.

Some Christians make bold to claim that they have actually taken their leave of God, while retaining some affiliation with what they consider to be a Christian ethic, quite independent of any commitment to faith in Jesus of Nazareth as the Christ of God. The obvious question here is: why do we still call them "Christians" then? The honest answer is that the title "Christian" is not ours to confer or to deny. The gospel that calls us to be vigilant also warns us not to be judgmental. To claim to have taken one's leave of God is not identical with the claim to have taken one's leave of the church.

Some people maintain a posture of intellectual skepticism, in keeping with their social stature as independent thinkers or academic achievers. They hold fast to a position of what they would call "benign agnosticism." Still others are overwhelmed by the strong arguments against a Christian theodicy—that is, the patient belief in a just, loving, and all-powerful God in the face of unjust, unexplained, and undeserved suffering.

Most Christians make some attempt to get around the charge of greed or avarice in this excessively materialistic culture by trying to reshape the mind of God, or to reinterpret the received word of God or, at least, to re-create God in their own image. God becomes for them the supreme pragmatist who sanctions such means as would result in the most favorable returns in power, wealth, prestige, and comfort. The God who was known to have called us to be faithful now seems to issue a fresh mandate to us to be successful.

Externally, the forces are also very strong. On the one hand, the concept of being a faithful servant to an unseen God just does not carry compelling weight with persons whose dominant image of themselves has to do with being served rather than to serve. It is just as untenable as the old-fashioned English governor on a poor Caribbean island who would end his letters to a poor old black lady with the words: "I have the honour to be, Madam, your obedient servant, John Smith, Governor." Neither the governor nor the addressee would ever dream of taking that seriously. For regardless of what Jesus might have said, to be the greatest was not thought to involve serving others. When one occupies the privileged position of being citizens of the only superpower left, one is more than likely to be guided by a "serve-us" rather than by a "service" mentality.[36] After all, what could Jesus really understand? He only came from Nazareth! Could anything good, or anyone great, come out of Nazareth? So being a servant in any form just does not fit the finest or noblest image we tend to have of ourselves.

On the other hand, we often presume to have the mastery over the systems and institutions by which we define and order our social relationships. We also presume to possess an unquestioned capacity to make right whatever seems to be wrong with them. And yet, this is the reality that lies very much at the heart of our postmodern dilemma. The President of Czechoslovakia, Vaclav Havel, commented on this in the following way:

> We are looking for new scientific recipes, new ideologies, new control systems, new institutions, new instruments to eliminate the dreadful consequences of our

previous recipes, ideologies, control systems, institutions and instruments. We treat the fatal consequences of technology as though they were a technical defect that could be remedied by technology alone. We are looking for an objective way out of the crisis of objectivism.

Everything would seem to suggest that this is not the way to go. We cannot devise, within the traditional modern attitude to reality, a system that will eliminate all the disastrous consequences of previous systems. We cannot discover a law or theory whose technical application will eliminate all the disastrous consequences of the technical application of earlier laws and technologies. What is needed is something different, something larger. Man's attitude to the world must be radically changed.[37]

Havel went on to call for a "sense of transcendental responsibility, archetypal wisdom, good taste, courage, compassion and faith in the importance of particular measures that do not aspire to be a universal key to salvation.[38]

The context in which we are called to serve is not only riddled with these internal and external forces of postmodernity, but it is also characterized by several areas of tension, some of which are creative and fertile, while others are debilitating and counter-productive. Let us look at some of these areas of tension.

First, there is the tension between *Neo-Fundamentalism* and *secular pragmatism*. There is little doubt that the champions of pragmatism, who have held sway in our techno-capitalistic culture for so long, have not really helped us to find the full meaning and happiness which was promised with material success. Furthermore, others are beginning to beat us at our own game by copying our tricks of the trade, and by following the same principles which have brought home the bacon for us for so long. Part of the response to all this has been an upsurge in the call for a return to basics, a call to rediscover the values of some mythical pristine era, to regenerate the mind-set of some earlier historical period when life was better, to reactivate some purer notions of living which were presumed to have been tried before. The tension here is not so much that of an either/or dilemma, but rather that of a both/and dilemma. The "Aha! Christians" who have just found Jesus and the Holy Spirit are finding great difficulty in selling all that they have to give to the poor, and then following Jesus into the Realm of God. They want to have their cake and eat it too!

Second, there is a major trend at work among some Christians that has been essentially borrowed from the world of economics. This is because there is a very close mental association made between the meaning of life and the essence of livelihood. That is to say, although we are told that humankind cannot live by bread alone, some insist that humankind cannot get very far without it. This means for them that life is always to be subjected to some form of cost-benefit analysis since it is the economic factor that constitutes the major paradigm of life. The tension for the Christian here is between the moral cost of discipleship and the material benefits to be derived from the so-called "good life." This is what I call the *theology of the bottom line*. Notions of sacrifice and simplicity, of self-emptying and modesty, which are inherent in the life of service, are often held hostage to more attractive notions of progress and profit.

Third, the theological tensions which have developed over the past three decades concerning the relationship between *orthodoxy* (right belief) and *orthopraxis* (right practice) have had a strong bearing on the contextual interpretations of service for the Christian. Prior to the rise of liberation theology, chiefly in Latin America, the earlier stirrings of the proponents of a political theology did not create such waves. Liberation theologians from Africa, Asia, and Latin America, and emancipatory theologians from the Caribbean and North America, have challenged the church to shift the emphasis away from mere orthodoxy, in terms of saying the thing right, toward a much more evangelical imperative of doing the right thing, and doing the thing right. Thus even the verb form of theology no longer consists in the speaking, but in the doing. We *do* theology, we *live* theology, we just do not speak it, let alone write it. This is not a revival of the old tension between faith and works, but rather a restatement of the tension between faith as dogma and faith as praxis.

Fourth, we can often detect a real tension between *divine consent* on the one hand, and *human consensus* on the other. It is the unconditional task of the Christian to seek to bring the workings of the human will into total harmony with the will of God. The obvious question is: how do we know what is the will of God? The question attributed to Saul of Tarsus on the Damascus road, "Lord, what wilt thou have me to do?" was never fully answered throughout the Apostle's lifetime. In many ways Paul manifested the truth of that voice from heaven which said that it was "hard to kick against the pricks" (to use the language of the King James Version), but he never stopped kicking anyhow!

The issue of human values is always complicated by the realities of our context, for what is taken to be normal among some Christians is quite demonic among others. Yet both claim divine sanction for their scale of values. The dilemma is not so much that we are not to serve two masters, but rather that God cannot be on both sides at the same time, and be God. So the question remains:

Whose side is God on? Or, is the voice of conscience the voice of God? Or, is the voice of the people the voice of God? In serving, whose voice shall we obey?

Fifth, we need to recognize that we now live in a world in which the term "charitable causes" has become much more a property of commerce and industry than it is of religion. It is just as bad as the term "act of God" becoming more the preserve of the insurance world. Charity is so loosely defined in our society that it is possible to be fully engaged in it with our time, talents, and money without becoming charitable ourselves. The options for participation in the so-called charitable causes are so numerous in our time that we need not go beyond the pull of enlightened self-interest to find a reason for supporting them. Benefactors often benefit more than beneficiaries. I call this the tension between *do-goodism* and *social righteousness.* Christian service is much more than do-goodism, for often the do-gooders constitute a barrier between the poor and the root causes of their poverty. Social righteousness takes the cause of God's justice seriously in God's created order, and seeks to remove the structures of injustice from the support of those who seek to do good in order to feel good. Christian service is about social transformation, not about structural affirmation. Do-goodism looks only at symptoms, while social righteousness looks at both symptoms and causes, and seeks to correct them.

Sixth, not only are we living in a radically new age, but we are increasingly being surrounded and attracted by the New Age movements. We can no longer pretend that they are not around. These movements include such groups as Adventures in Enlightenment, channeling, UFO's, ecofeminism, astrology, and Theosophy. They have the potential to attract many of our children and their children, especially when they genuinely believe that we have failed them for want of religious example. Professor

Ted Peters of Berkeley, California, has helped us greatly to
learn more about these movements in his book *The Cosmic
Self.* In it he explains that the "new age seeks to heal what
was previously the pain of separation."[39] He expresses his
sympathy for some of the values that the movement
teaches: "...world peace, inner peace, healing of division,
attention to personal experience, optimism about the
future, and cosmic consciousness." He also expresses his
criticism of it by saying: "[In] its haste to find personal bliss
by identifying the self with the cosmos, the new age has
inadvertently fallen into a gnostic form of spiritual quest
(which) naively assumes that if we can think better, then
reality will somehow be better. New age gnosticism fails to
accept the full reality and pervasiveness of sin and brokenness; and it likewise denies the reality of God's grace in
the work of salvation.[40] Whether the New Age movement is
demonic or divine is really not for us to judge, for
Christianity itself was once a new age movement in the
Roman Empire. What we must recognize, however, is that
the blatant gaps which we so comfortably sustain between
what we preach and what we practice are among the most
generative elements of New Age converts.

We have been looking at some of the contextual realities of our time, and at some of the forces at work in the
sphere into which we are called to follow Christ and to
serve for the sake of the gospel. These factors and forces
are often beyond our capacity to control, or even to
clearly define. Yet we certainly encounter them in this
world into which we are called and sent by God. We need
to turn therefore to look at what being the servant means
in such a time and context as this.

From Serving to Servanthood

The New Testament offers us a wide range of usage for the term "to serve." This creates something of a problem for us when we try to determine what constitutes true servanthood. In fact there are eight different Greek verbs employed in the New Testament. They are: *diakoneo* (Acts 6:2), to serve at table; *douleo* (Lk 16:13), to serve as a slave; *latreuo* (Mt 4:10), to serve for wages; *hypereteo* (Acts 13:36), to serve as rower; *paredreuo* (1 Cor. 9:13), to serve as one who sits by constantly; *therapeuo* (Acts 17:25), to serve as healer; *prosecho* (Heb 7:13), to serve attentively; *leitourgeo* (Heb 10:11), to serve the church or state.

What shall we do with all these words since the English language merely provides us with one? Should we anglicize each word into an adjective or adverb, and use them alongside the English verb or noun, such as "diakonal"? Should we choose some of them and ignore the others? Or should we take the deepest hints from the language of, and about, Jesus in the New Testament? If we stick to the notion of service as the essence of discipleship, then perhaps we should select some of the words that suit our tastes and convenience, and pretend that the others are not important. If we choose to anglicize the Greek verbs to indicate our particular meaning at the time, then we run the risk of compartmentalizing the vocation to which we have been called. This would just be as simplistic as qualifying God's love and the Christian's love as "agape" love, as if "eros" were concocted in some extraterrestrial laboratory.

The gospels tell us that *diakoneo* is the verb which Jesus mainly uses. Service is *diakonia* in the fellowship of the Realm of God, and it is chiefly the service of each other. We are to serve at each other's tables, says Jesus, and to wash each other's feet. But Paul speaks of himself as the slave of Christ, the *doulos*, and he calls on Christians to see themselves only in that light: *to kurio Christo douleuete,* "you serve the Lord Christ" (Col 3:24). The writer of the Letter of James is the slave of God and of the Lord Jesus Christ (Jas 1:1). Peter is a slave and apostle of Jesus Christ (2 Pt 1:1).

Much more significant however is the Philippian Hymn of Christ—Phil 2:5–11—in which Jesus is said to empty himself, taking the form of a slave, a *doulos,* being born in the likeness of men. There can be little doubt that the image and profile of the Suffering Servant of Deutero-Isaiah is very much in the picture here. For not only does the early church make the connection with Jesus as the Christ, and as the Suffering Servant, but the church also appropriates the full weight and meaning of what it means to be in Christ as a part of the new creation. The new creation is slavery in Christ.

It is now no longer simply *diakoneo,* but *douleo.* Fellow servants in the Lord are also slaves of Christ at the same time. The church, then, is not merely a band of slaves; it is a hard-working community, singing together in the heat of the world's sun, trying to make the work lighter for each fellow servant, just as the Haitians do. It is trying to make full use of the many gifts (charisms) with which God has so richly endowed it. The band of slaves for Christ is also the servant community, and servanthood takes on a much deeper meaning than mere service. A waiter changes his uniform after he has served the last table, and is no longer a waiter for the time being. But the slave remains a slave by night and by day, regardless of the change of clothing, wholly owned by the One who has called him into servanthood. Ronald Sunderland has rightly said that "servanthood is not an attribute that may be confined to selected corners of one's life; it is all-encompassing in its reach and application.[41]

The church as a servant community then is understood in the New Testament to have been given certain tasks. Some of these tasks have a direct bearing on the nature of servanthood, while others seem to have a direct bearing on the challenge of Christian friendship, which we will discuss in our next chapter. Among the specific tasks for the church to be mentioned in the category of servanthood are: *kerygma,* preaching; *didache,* teaching; *leitourgia,* worship; *diakonia,* serving; *oikonomia,* stewardship. In each of these tasks the New Testament seems to be clear about the ontological nature of the disciple. The disciple *is* a servant, called to be fully engaged in the total and faithful proclamation of the gospel, not only by preaching, but also by the other functions that are essential to good servanthood. So that even the task of *leitourgia,* which we translate as worship, is actually a term from the workplace, and not from the worship-space. The truly liturgical person is not the one who worships correctly, but the one who works faithfully. Perhaps we need to be more intent on serving a Christ who died on a cross between two thieves, and not between two candlesticks.

When we take yet another look at the four marks of the church, what can they tell us about ourselves as members of a servant community? How do the four marks of the church characterize the meaning of servanthood? First, the *unity* of the church, which reminds us of the oneness of the Body of Christ, also points to God's own self-giving. To share in Christ's Body is to share in God's Sacrament, the church. Servanthood is therefore sacramental in nature. It is an outward and visible manifestation of an inward and spiritual relationship, freely initiated by God, sustained through the indwelling of God's Spirit, and making us ever ready to bring forth the fruit of good works. The sacramental community is also the servant community, for God's call and God's self-giving are identical, and we dare not kidnap the sacrament and run away from the servanthood.

Second, the mark of *holiness* that tells us about the very character of Godself, also tells us about the character of God's household, the church. "You shall be holy for I am holy," says the Lord. The church as God's household is the Holy Church, and the servant of Christ is God's steward in God's household. Servanthood is stewardship then. Stewardship involves trust, commitment, and accountability to the One who has entrusted the church to us. It involves the readiness to accept and understand the limitations of that trust, and the undying need to be trustworthy. Servanthood as stewardship will always involve a constant updating of the catalog of gifts with which one has been entrusted. For sometimes the nature of the gifts changes; sometimes the gifts are withdrawn without our notice, even if we are reluctant to admit it. It must always remain true that the Lord who gives is also the Lord who takes away. Thus the steward not only maintains a *sense of vocation* but also a *sense of occasion.* We know when to, and when not to. We know how far, and how long. We know the time and the season for everything, or almost everything.

Third, we come again to the *catholicity* of the church. This is a mark that defines its obligation to proclaim the whole Christian faith to all people the world over until the end of time. The church is catholic because it is a community of those who have been set free by God through Christ—the community of those whose new life in Christ transcends culture, confronts history, and transforms the meaning of human existence. It is new life in the Christ who came not to be served but to serve, and to give his life as a ransom for many (Mk 10:45). To share in that life as servant then is to be a living symbol of the One who serves and sets free. For servanthood, catholicity means symbol.

The servant is a living symbol of the One whom he/she serves, for the essence of that symbol is that it participates actively in that which it seeks to represent.

The servant then is a living symbol of freedom, justice, goodness, sacrifice, faithfulness, and transforming love. We are living symbols insofar as we seek to imitate Christ by serving others as Christ did, and by seeking to offer ourselves and our service in the cause of bringing in the Realm of God. Servanthood as symbol is not just about doing good works, it is also about being good persons for the sake of Christ and the salvation of the world. Christian symbolism reminds us constantly that who we are often speaks more loudly than all that we do. As servants of Christ we strive to be living symbols of integration, the integration of the gospel story with the personal story, the sacred sphere with the secular, ultimate reality with intimate experience, the now with the not-yet. We strive somehow to become what we are already.

Fourth, the *apostolicity* of the church means that it is to continue in the teaching and fellowship of the apostles of Jesus Christ, and that it is sent to carry out and sustain the mission of Christ to everyone. The church is apostolic because it is the contemporary heir of those first smelly and unlettered fishermen—radical activists and confused young men who made some weird claims about their good friend and leader who had been eliminated by the powerful. They claimed that he was alive, that they had really seen him, and that he had charged them not to go back on their recent experiences and on what he had told them. Their claims have stuck even down to today. Apostolicity has as much to do with succession as with progression. It means to make sure that the claims of Peter and his gang keep sticking. Apostolicity then calls on servanthood to be a living sign that the old claims are true, that they can be relied on, and that the more people accept them the better it will be for the whole world. Servanthood as a sign means the living out of a genuinely distinguishing witness in the world that the gospel is real. It is a sign of the Realm of God. It is a warning against evil. It is a concrete assurance that God is still around and active. It is a call and a challenge to others to come and join. It is a human placard writ large in current consciousness, not only that the church has something to say, but that the church really believes what it says. Servants of Christ are called to be conspicuous signs that, in their own lives, the church is unswervingly committed to that for which God has called it into being. They affirm that the Realm of God is surely on the way, and that they themselves are a guaranteed foretaste of what it is really all about. What they see is really what they will get. Sunderland rightly states that: "The character of servanthood compels the servant to live as an exemplar of living service, and the community of servants as the first fruits of the society so created.[42]

Christian servanthood as a living sign is most powerfully expressed as we seek to provide moral leadership and faithful witness in a world that has lost its way, and clearly does not know how to find it. Our lives must proclaim that the apostolic church has not lost its way. Ours is the task to strive to be leaders and not followers in the restoration of the love of God in the hearts, lives, and faces of all who come in contact with us. They must come to us because we have been advertising through our church life that we have been with Jesus. We must be careful not to advertise as being living signs if we are not prepared to deliver the goods—moral, spiritual, social.

From Servanthood to Servanting

Who takes the lead in the business of Christian servant-hood? Is the order based on race, or class, or status, or nationality, or belief? Does the context alter the command to serve?

I am really not sure how to answer any of these questions intelligently. I only know that the main issue here has to do with making a shift away from *doing* toward an emphasis on *becoming,* and with making a critical decision no longer to maintain any distance between who we are and what we do. As Christians, we are expected to be in the business, not of saying we are servants, but of serving— and of moving from servanthood to servanting. For those who seek to take being slaves of Christ seriously, "servant-hood" could still remain static, whereas "servanting" could only become increasingly dynamic. The issue involves a movement away from just *being* toward the daily process of *becoming* when we are in service with Christ. Servanthood is singular, but servanting is corporate. Who serves first therefore serves best, because they lead others into a closer relationship with the very meaning of their faith and the call to true Christian discipleship.

Servanting means being transformed into the image of the image of God. For too long we have played politics with that very central term of Genesis 1:26, 27 that we are created in the image and likeness of God. The *imago dei* means so many things to so many different persons, depending on what they really want to say. The *Carmen Christi* (Song of Christ) of Philippians 2 is quite clear. So too is the message of Colossians 1. Jesus is the image of the invisible God, and Jesus in human fashion takes the form of a slave. It is the life and death of Jesus of Nazareth that alone untarnishes and restores the reality and efficacy of the image of God. Irenaeus speaks of a *recapitulation,* a summing up of everything in Christ. Christians must seek no other way of appropriating that image of God, but must rather seek to be transformed into the image of that very image by taking the form of a slave as well. If we do not like it we should leave it. There can be no other. *Christus Rex* (Christ the King) is truly *Christus Crucifixus* (Christ Crucified), and we dare not destroy the cruciality of the cross by obscuring the stripped and suffering slave of God with kingly robes and golden crown.

Servanting means engaging in a radically new way of interpreting what it means to be "in Christ." We say with Paul that Christ lives in us. We need to go on to say that the Christ who lives in us is also the Christ who serves through us. This therefore requires what I call a prepositional shift from being servants *of* Christ to being servants *with* Christ. Servanting then is not just being *servants of* but becoming *servants with* Christ. As Christian slaves Christ never leaves us to serve all by ourselves, for he has promised to be with us always. To serve in the name of Christ carries much more than a mere memory of our Christian calling, it involves mystical collaboration with the One who is always on the way with us.

This is what is meant by Christopraxis. I entirely agree with Jurgen Moltmann in his book, *The Way of Jesus Christ,* when he states that Christopraxis must be understood as the "life of the community of Christians in the discipleship of Jesus" and not just the application of a theory about Christ.

> It is a way of life, a way in which people who learn who Jesus is, learn it with all their senses, acting and suffering, in work and prayer....It means learning to know him in the praxis of discipleship.... Christopraxis inevitably leads the community of Christ to the poor, the sick, to "surplus people" and

to the oppressed.... As the Christ for all human beings, Jesus takes hold of our divided and peaceless human society at its lowest point, among the miserable, the despised and the unimportant.[43]

In other words, servanting means making our Haitian refugees and neighbors a top priority. We dare not head for heaven without them.

Servanting demands the deliberate declericalization of ministry and servanthood, and the imaginative identification and stimulation of the many gifts which God makes available, both within the church and without. Servanting means stirring up divine gifts wherever they can be found. In their historic pastoral letter, *But We See Jesus,* the black Episcopal Bishops urged their church along these lines:

> We therefore wish to urge most strongly, that every effort should be made to mobilize the talents and gifts which God is making available to us in all of our members, and that the clergy in particular should do everything in their power to encourage and strengthen the work of the laity, even in innovative and more imaginative ways. We do not believe that evangelism and stewardship can be either effective or fertile if participation is stifled and lay ministry is suppressed. Let no part of the Body of Christ say to the other, "I have no need of you."[44]

Finally, servanting means becoming a living, working, and witnessing doxology in which we praise as we servant, and in servanting more, we offer up more praise. It is not only the work of the servant but also the life of the servant that must constitute an unambiguous doxology in itself. To serve is to praise and to praise is to serve. This is why we go back to the world of the psalter: "Praise the

Lord, praise the name of the Lord, give praise, O servants of the Lord, you that stand in the house of the Lord, in the courts of the house of our God" (Ps 135:1–2). In all of this, *leitourgia* is joined with *douleia* in servanting, and slavery and liturgy come together in doxology. It is only in the faithful servanting of God that we find perfect freedom. Listen to the servants of God when they get together to praise:

> *The law of the Lord is perfect,*
> *reviving the soul;*
> *The testimony of the Lord is sure,*
> *making wise the simple.*
> *The precepts of the Lord are right,*
> *rejoicing the heart.*
> *The commandment of the Lord is clear,*
> *enlightening the eyes.*
> *The fear of the Lord is pure,*
> *enduring forever.*
> *The ordinances of the Lord are true,*
> *and righteous altogether;*
> *More to be desired are they than gold,*
> *even much fine gold,*
> *Sweeter also than honey*
> *and drippings of the honeycomb.*
> *Moreover by them is thy servant warned;*
> *in keeping them there is great reward.*
> *Let the words of my mouth*
> *and the meditation of my heart,*
> *be acceptable in thy sight,*
> *O Lord, my rock and my redeemer.*
> (Ps 19:7–11,14)

If we are prepared to serve the Lord with gladness, not only by coming within God's presence with songs of praise, but also by immersing ourselves in God's world as slaves with Christ, then we must also be prepared to serve as each other's friends rather than as competitors for a scarce supply of prizes or rewards. The slave of Christ is also the slave with Christ. The slave with Christ is also the one whom Jesus calls his friend. It is therefore to a discussion on the meaning of friendship in Christian discipleship and ministry to which we must turn our attention in the next chapter.

CHAPTER FIVE

THE MINISTRY
OF FRIENDSHIP

MANY PEOPLE HAVE ASKED WHAT AMERICA WILL DO without an enemy, now that the Soviet Union is no more. Can America survive without one? Can a country whose basic economy is shaped by the sword ever transform itself by means of the plowshare? Now that the communists are disappearing, do we not need another enemy for the promotion of our national resolve and consummate patriotism? We lost one in Noriega, in Gaddafi, in Saddam Hussein. Can we find one in China or in Yugoslavia? Should we look for one among ourselves? Suppose the real enemy is us; what shall we do?

During any season of national elections in the United States, adversarial politics usually takes center stage. Little molehills become towering Everests. Bones long buried are excavated for their devastating worth. Simple and honest mistakes are rekindled in the fiery furnaces of political expediency. America relishes it all, as human dignity and decency are sacrificed on the altars of the lust for power. This is the climate in which we choose our public leaders. This is how we seek to consign ourselves to the texts of global history.

What does it really mean when America claims to be "One Nation Under God"? If it is the politics of hatred that delivers the goods, why should we shift to the soft options in the politics of love? In the public sphere, the politics of love is not bankable. It does not create wealth. It does not harness the strongest human forces by which material progress is assured. Hatred creates aggression, and aggression stirs competition, and competition produces winners, and winning is the name of the game—in war, commerce, education, politics, leisure, family life, and yes, even in religion.

Vincent Harding in his book *Hope and History* tells of his attraction to a book title, *Is America Possible?* as he wrestled with the problems of America's social pathos. He uses that as a theme for reflecting on Langston Hughes's famous poem, "Let America Be America Again," written in 1935. Harding comments that the poem is "its own commentary and encouragement." He quotes this verse, for example, "O, let America be America again-/ The land that never has been yet-/ And yet must be-/ The Land where every man is free."[45] Harding muses on the hopes, dreams, and expectations that one day all Americans will enjoy the same freedoms that are enshrined in their Constitution. He wonders still if any of this will ever come to pass. Is America possible? he asks himself. My question is simply this: Is Christianity possible in America? When we make our living from the calculus of hatred and competition, can we still create new life from the calculus of love and community? A colleague of mine has posed this question: Can one be a good American, a good black, and a good Christian at the same time? Many there are who would have difficulty in giving an honest answer.

If Christianity is a religion of love, is Christianity possible in a culture that cannot survive without an enemy? Who are we to love then? The gospel calls for enemy-love, but that is culturally unhealthy. If it is culturally unhealthy to love the enemy, can we love those who are not our enemies? What about those with whom we share faith and worship, those whom we call the "dearly beloved" in our churches? Can we really love the dearly beloved? Can we honestly share friendship with those who share faith with us? This is what the discussion in this chapter is about. What are the terms of endearment for those of us who dare to be Christian?

We have already attempted to explore the implications of being members of the church as the disciple-community, for Christian ministry is essentially that faithful discipleship of Christ in a filial relationship with God. Those who claim a filial relationship with the One God also share a relationship with each other. Can we have a filial relationship with God without a working relationship with each other?

We have also tried to explore the meaning of this working relationship with Christ and each other, as members of the servant-community, the church, and the existential imperatives of Christian servanting. Can there be a genuinely Christian working relationship in a hostile and friendless environment? Is the servant-community more than just a concourse of servants? Can it also be a community of those who serve each other, because they are both friends of Jesus and friends of each other? Or, on the other hand, is it possible to be a friend of Jesus without being a friend of his other friends? Can we have it both ways?

Let us turn then to examine what we can make of the church as a community-of-friends, for that is what Jesus said he would prefer to call us: friends. "I do not call you servants any longer,...but I have called you friends, because I have made known to you everything that I have heard from my Father. You did not choose me, but I chose you"

(Jn 15:15,16). How can the church, as a social institution, take seriously this preferred status of mutual friendship to which Jesus summons us in the gospel?

Is the church simply a function of the society as a whole? Does it mirror the society with all of its traits and problems, or just some of its problems? What sort of social immunity does the church enjoy, in the face of our common social habits and expectations? Robert Bellah and his colleagues offer the following critique of our institutions:

> It is easy to see this as a personal problem, to say that Americans have become selfish, self-indulgent, spoiled by affluence and readily available goods: or as a cultural problem, to say that we have lost the work ethic and have come to believe that the good life is a life of hedonism and comfort. But we want to argue that it is also, and perhaps primarily, an institutional problem. Our institutions today—from the family to the school to the corporation to the public arena—do not challenge us to use all our capacities so that we have a sense of enjoyable achievement and of contributing to the welfare of others.[46]

Does the church fall within this category as well? Is the church as an institution a part of the social disease, while all along it purports to be a significant part of the cure? In spite of its highly structured and institutional framework, we still insist that the church is essentially a community of communities. Let us explore what this means.

Community of Communities

Although we have spoken of the church as a disciple-community, and as a servant-community, we still need to grapple with the fact that the church is still a community *among* communities, struggling to be the community *of* communities. We often make a distinction between the gathered church and the scattered church, in terms of worship and witness respectively. But it is very much the case that our scatteredness is hardly ever challenged or transformed in our gathering. Far from leaving behind our ordinary connections of class or social groupings when we gather, we more often expect to have those several identities reaffirmed and baptized. The song in our hearts simply says: "Don't try to change us / Nor rearrange us!"

Bellah and his colleagues speak in terms of the "public church." They describe our multiple loyalties, and contend that our religious loyalty transcends our national loyalty. They speak about the powerful institutions in the country which influence our lives and absorb so much of our energies. They describe these as follows: "They seem to pressure us to compete for individual advantage rather than to combine for the common welfare, and they empty out meaning from our lives when they structure our existence as a competitive race for money, power, prestige, or the consumer goods that symbolize them."[47]

It seems to me that a crucial aspect of this dilemma in the church community has to do with the reasons for the practice of religion itself. The gathered church is also the gathering of competing needs and agendas. While some practice their religion out of a sense of habit, or duty, or personal need, others do not disguise their quest for power, or profit, or social mobility. There are varying religious habits that I group as being represented by the church shoppers, church hoppers, and church droppers. Although our churches are to be bastions of love and mercy, we yet feel the full blast of the winds of competition, rivalry, hostility, mutual misunderstandings, interest cliques, and self-righteous manipulation. Furthermore, the clash of theologies that often characterize the moral, liturgical, and political controversies in the church is a direct symptom of the root differences in the meaning and function of religion itself. The battle between right and right is often much fiercer than that between right and wrong; and the church is often the battleground for the former.

Another aspect of our dilemma revolves around some critical tensions involved in four dimensions of the church's social function. *One,* there is the tension between the church that is called by God to be actively engaged in the process of social transformation, and the church that merely concerns itself with a disengaged witness and lifestyle. *Two,* there is the tension between the primacy of evangelism as an inescapable duty of the church, and the simple need for a renewal of individual faith and witness. *Three,* the theology of the mission of God is often in conflict with the actual mission of the church, even when we say that it is God's church. The symbol of the cross offers the world a radically different message from the symbol of the crown, but the church often wears the latter while it strides liturgically behind the former. *Four,* the challenge of ecumenism for Christians, which is often supported by the sense of "One Lord, One Faith, One Baptism," comes up against the realities of power and the ethos of pluralism—whether cultural, social, or theological. Too often we are tempted to adopt compromises which override the ecumenical imperatives of the gospel.

How does the church measure up as a community of communities, when faced with such realities? What are the signs of hope? To what does it cling for meaning and a stronger sense of identity and direction? I see a few signs of real hope within the church. Among them I would include the following: a) The gradual emancipation of Christian theology; it is no longer the exclusive preserve of the theologians; b) the serious participation of the younger generations; c) the increased formation and involvement of the laity in the church's praxis and leadership; d) the adoption of greater initiative and responsibility for outreach and service; e) the confronting of, exposure to, and elimination of prejudice and cultural bondage within congregations and seminaries; f) the rediscovery of justice as a centrifugal paradigm for Christian witness; g) the growing acknowledgment of the need for greater simplicity through force of circumstances. These signs of hope are really growth points in the church, as it struggles to come to grips with being a community of communities.

No other concept offers the church greater anchorage as the community of communities than the meaning of the Realm of God. The church is the community that is called to live out in postmodern society the interconnectedness between Jesus and the Realm, the church and the Realm, the world and the Realm. This is because the Jesus who once proclaimed the Realm of God is now proclaimed by the church as the Realm.

What does this Realm of God mean for us today, especially if the church is to be understood as the community of the Realm? It is certainly not to be equated with any form of aristocracy, democracy, christocracy, or theocracy on earth. The Realm of God breaks in on history, but it also transcends it. In 1938 Paul Tillich defined the Realm (Kingdom) of God as a "dynamic power acting in history, materializing itself in history although never becoming identical with history."[48] He further described it as the "dynamic fulfillment of the ultimate meaning of existence against the contradictions of existence." We have already been observing some of the contradictions of existence in the life of our Christian vocation in this culture. Wolfhart Pannenberg, in 1967, described the Kingdom (Realm) of God as "that perfect society of men which is to be realized in history by God himself."[49] I have some difficulties with this approach by Pannenberg because of the ease with which he makes history become the sphere for the realization of God's perfect order. While it is true that we must make no dichotomy between world history and salvation history, it is also true that salvation involves more than the perfection of world order. It is either that something more is required of history, or that we reappropriate the meaning of the Realm of God on which Jesus based his proclamation and ministry.

I have found that the Dutch theologian, Anton Houtepen, has offered us a more appealing descriptive phrase. He says: "The Kingdom of God is a principle of action, the starting point for thought and action, through which the person is addressed, and others begin to look aslant across the way things happen in society and act differently."[50] It is the phrase "aslant across" that I find so significant, for the church becomes a community of communities not so much by its inclusiveness, but rather by its capacity to make a diagonal slice across all existing communities, and thus to embrace them differently. Bruce Chilton and J. I. H. McDonald also contribute to this line of thinking with their assertion that: "The Kingdom of God intersects the course of human history and experience. It is realized par excellence not in the dream world of apocalyptic nor in temple cult, legalistic casuistry, ascetic discipline nor power politics, but in personal and community life that is responsive to the call of God. Such intersection promotes a distinctive way of life that has a transcendent horizon and a faith-dynamic."[51] Again, it is that "transcendent horizon" which offers the church the greatest opportunity to become the community of communities, and thus the community of the Kingdom.

As the community of the Realm of God, the church is in a continuous process of unfolding, revealing, proclaiming the mystery of God as the creating, emancipatory, and sustaining presence in the world. That divine presence is concretely affirmed in the diverse conditions of humanity within it, and such an internal pluralism is not the result of a divine mistake, nor does it constitute a threat to the saving will of God, as some people might suggest by their religious and social prejudices. The pluralism within the church is often seen as a threat to order and preferred discipline. Many bemoan the fact that there are high-church people with a low doctrine of society, and low-church people with a high doctrine of society, and some who have no doctrine at all. The internal pluralism is not merely among individuals, it is also within individuals. Thus conflict often precipitates the consent of the church, and consensus hardly prevails for long. Yet it is still an instrument of God's grace to the world; it is still God's gift in the new creation. The church is not the Realm of God, but it is a community of that Realm, with all the paradox and ambiguity which divine mystery and unmerited grace inevitably force on our simple human minds. We affirm what we do not fully understand. The challenge is for us to act out in Realm-of-God fashion what we have already been affirming, namely, that the community of the Realm is a foretaste of heaven, and that heavenly culture is based on love not hatred, on self-giving not self-interest, on looking for the friend even in the worst enemy. "If your enemy is hungry, feed him; or thirsty, give him a drink" (Rom 12:20).

As a community of the Realm of God, the church is committed to the evangelical task of proclaiming the gospel of Jesus in terms of the oneness of the whole human family, not just in terms of the unity of the church. If the evangelical task is to be truly ecumenical and Spirit-driven, then God's *oikoumene,* God's inhabited earth, cannot be coterminous with the church, but rather with humanity wherever it is to be found. This means that the selective ecumenism that is practiced by some groups of Christians stands under the constant judgment of the Realm of God. It also means that those who are of other faiths, and with whom we claim to share a common origin, must somehow be embraced as faith-cousins, rather than as anonymous Christians, or as resident aliens, or as sophisticated heathens. If it is true for us that there can never be a single soul for whom Jesus Christ has not died, it must also be true for our Muslim cousins that there is not a single soul on whom Allah can have no mercy. The community of the Realm of God does not limit its terms of endearment and friendship to persons of like faith.

As a community of the Realm of God, the church seeks to bear witness to the belief that Christ is the center of history. In so doing, it will concretely neutralize all that is destructive of the human spirit, and confront all the "meaning-defying powers of existence," to use Tillich's phrase. Thus it would seek to avoid the danger of which William Willimon warns: "A Church that expends too much energy leaning over to speak to the world sometimes falls in."[52] The community of the Realm of God best take its political task seriously, through a critical reflection on its own mission, message, and common life, and thereby pursue its critical and prophetic vocation to the wider society. The community of the Realm of God can thus challenge the socio-economic, cultural, ideological, and political heritages of our times toward their transformation into instruments of life that are fully human. The community of the Realm of God can demonstrate faithfully that human rights are more than legal conventions. They are the demands of the divine right to be human. They are also the rights of demand by others on our own humanity. In this community, love is not a *maybe*, love is a *must*—that is the nature of the new commandment in the new creation. We must, at the very least, be about the business of loving the dearly beloved. For it cannot be that we would seek to be agents of change in a sinful and naughty world, while we resist being changed ourselves.

As a community of the Realm of God, the church is formed by a sense of the vision of God *in* the world. Thus would it seek not to re-create God in its own image. We dare not give further comfort to the remark once made by the French philosopher Voltaire, who said that "if God made us in His image, we have certainly returned the compliment."[53] We must faithfully bear witness to that God who continues to call us away from our brokenness. This means, for example, that when the church gives support to structures of injustice and oppression, of male dominance and white supremacy, of North Atlantic power and technocracy, some of the victims are forced to ask whether God is real. For them, it seems, it is a very strange coincidence that such a God always seems so powerless to alter the social structures in order to make life less intolerable for the oppressed. Why, they ask, are the same people poor all the time? They also ask whose side God is on. It is inherent in the life of the community of the Realm of God that the true vision of God must not only form, but must also transform, the people of God.

The community of communities, then, is not only the community of the Realm of God, with all the implications we have just been outlining; it is also the waiting community, the anticipatory community, living out what it means by its claim to be the character of heaven on earth. The anticipatory community is a community of love and friendship. Can it become a communion of friends? Let us see what this means.

Friendly Community?
Or Communion of Friends?

The history of the Quaker movement tells us that George Fox and his colleagues were guided by Jesus' designation of his disciples as "friends," in John 15:14: "You are my friends if you do what I command you." They wanted to give primary emphasis to the spiritual experience of what it meant to be faithful followers of Jesus; and they did not see how they could be friends of Jesus without being friends of each other. Thus were they known as the Society of Friends. Their patient and quiet support of the emancipation of the Negro is well known in American history, for to be friends of Jesus was to be friends of the Negro. Among themselves, it could be said of the Quakers that "they feel the terrible pull of the unlimited liability for one another which the New Testament ethic lays upon them."[54]

It is this significant phrase, "unlimited liability," which truly marked the relationship between Jesus and his followers: "Greater love has no man than this, that a man lay down his life for his friends" (Jn 15:13). The cross is not only the supreme symbol of the love of God, it is also the ultimate demonstration of human friendship. Christianity was born out of a love between one man and his friends, a love that was not severed by his death. The church that emerged out of their friendship assumed certain tasks. Each task was intrinsically related to sustaining that shared friendship in the Spirit, through their incorporation into Christ. These tasks included *koinonia*—fellowship, or mutual participation; *marturia*—common witness; *therapeia*—healing, or making whole; *oikodoumene*—edification, or the building up of the household of God. Each task made it necessary for the disciples to be friends, to share an unlimited liability in bearing each other's burdens, in suffering with those who suffered, and rejoicing with those who rejoiced.

Thus every New Testament image of the church sought to give further expression to the meaning of Christian friendship—whether in prayer or praise, whether in service or suffering.

What is Christian friendship, then? Is friendship the same thing as friendliness? Friendliness is easy, it is produced on demand. Friendship is costly, it is not readily attained. Friendly faces may warm the heart, but the loving heart creates the friend. What does the church have to do with friendliness? Is it to create a happy feeling within its environment, against the surrounding unfriendliness in the world? Stanley Hauerwas has said: "The called church has become the voluntary church, whose primary characteristic is that the congregation is friendly. Of course, this is a kind of discipline, because you cannot belong to a church unless you are friendly, but it's very unclear how such friendliness contributes to the growth of God's church meant to witness to the kingdom of God."[55] The community of the Realm of God is not about compromise, complacency, or feeling good; it is about using the sword of the Spirit and wearing the breastplate of righteousness. It is not called to be a friendly community; it is called to be a communion of friends of Jesus the Friend. Friendly communities seek to gain the world; the communion of friends seeks to save the world. Certain implications flow from this.

First, when my ARCIC II (Anglican/Roman Catholic International Commission II) colleagues and I were wrestling for over three years with our second Agreed Statement on *The Church as Communion,* we focused attention on the meaning of *communio* as an area of convergence between Roman Catholics and Anglicans. We stated that the church was the sacrament of God; the church was the Gift of God; we pointed to the shared fruit of the Spirit (Gal 5:22, 23) within the church; we laid great emphasis on the central meaning of the eucharist in the life of the communion. Yet we failed to go further to deal with the church as a communion of friends, to draw out the ecumenical imperatives of *communio* as spiritual, emotional, personal, reciprocal friendship. We failed to draw to the attention of our churches the inherent challenge of commitment in communion, and to make plain that Christian friendship in diversity is a faithful response to the creative will of God. As representative theologians we were very friendly towards each other, but we refused to risk eucharistic friendship at the Lord's table, or to call on our churches to give concrete and sacramental expression to our shared friendship of God in the Body of Christ. I am increasingly convinced that the more hopeful way forward is to begin with an ecumenism "from below." We must act out that friendship which has already been given to us through the Spirit, rather than adopt a posture of theological friendliness through documents and clichés.

Second, when we look even further at the four marks of the church—unity, holiness, catholicity, and apostolicity—there are some more practical applications to which we are pointed in our self-understanding as a communion of friends. Not only do we take on board the three Christian virtues of faith, hope, and love; we also seek to embrace the theological significance of the so-called cardinal virtues: justice, temperance, courage, and prudence. In the economy of Christian praxis, catholicity demands courage, apostolicity demands prudence, holiness demands temperance, and unity demands justice. In the context of exploring the church as the communion of friends, let us look at the unity of the church as expressive of the unitive love of God. Friendship that is based on the love of God also requires justice, it never replaces it. The Roman Catholic theologian, Walter Kasper, has powerfully stated that love requires justice and practices it. It confers the proper vision through which to discern the changing requirements of justice in the changing conditions of society. It perceives unjust conditions, criticizes them, and motivates people to overcome them. Love is the soul of justice, so to speak. But love also outbids the demands of justice, so it is only love which leads to a truly human order, in which there is friendship, forgiveness, solidarity, and the readiness to help other people.[56]

Third, there is a practical, yet mystical, reality that is inherent in our friendship with God. For, in this regard, we recall that it is on God's invitation that our friendship with God is created and sustained. "You did not choose me, but I chose you." I agree with Isabel Anders in her book, *The Faces of Friendship,* when she says: "Friendship with God, in Christ, is a pervasive occupation of the Christian, and all other relationships and activities are somehow to be found in the light of that commitment."[57] Anders goes on to remind us that it is a work of the Spirit, "a connection with the life of God that is granted to us, that comes down to us as life flows from the branch to the vines."[58] Several years ago, C. S. Lewis had put it somewhat differently in his little classic, *The Four Loves:* Friendship is

> the instrument by which God reveals to each the beauties of all the others. They are no greater than the beauties of a thousand other men; by Friendship God opens our eyes to them. They are, like all beauties, derived from Him, and then, in a good Friendship, increased by Him through the Friendship itself, so that it is His instrument of creating as well as for revealing."[59]

Nothing can be more powerful than to recognize in our frail and human existence that sense of the creative love of God, through which in our friendships as Christians we are instruments of God's transforming and sanctifying grace.

Fourth, to live in the communion of friends demands that the many factors of friendship be addressed. These obviously involve complementarity, patience, mutual respect, openness, interdependence, vulnerability, self-giving, personal clarity, maturity, solidarity, accountability, faithfulness, compassion, and the search for equality. To live in the communion of friends demands a basic friendship with oneself, by accepting oneself in the same measure by which one learns to accept God's acceptance of ourselves, and others, in love and solidarity. To live in the communion of friends demands a life of intimacy. Such intimacy does not threaten the personhood of the other, nor does it invade the spiritual and emotional identity of the other. It does not give grandeur to the power of feeling, nor prominence to the urges of domination and conquest. Rather, it seeks to celebrate the fullness of God's gift of life as a shared spiritual experience and, by the guidance of God's Spirit, it enables true friendship to blossom as the sign of wholesome love in a world of self-centered brokenness. The politics of sexuality will only be neutralized by the sweet grace of divine intimacy. Let the church learn to love as friends and not to live as aliens. Let us see what such loving, as friends, can suggest, if we commit ourselves to the task of loving those with whom God has called us to worship and witness together.

Covenanting for Friendship

We have spoken of the church as the communion of friends. We need to remember that it is also the covenant community, that which is called into being as a result of the new covenant of Jesus Christ. The ancient people of Israel understood themselves to be in covenant with the God who had emancipated them from the bondage of Egypt. We Christians, as the New Israel, understand the resurrection of Christ to be the new exodus, and that through baptism our incorporation into Christ means entry into a new covenantal relationship.

Our eucharistic fellowship in the body and blood of the new covenant is either a gigantic pantomime, or it is genuine table friendship, truly symbolic of who we would really love to become. It is either that we make eucharist on Sundays, and at other times, for dramatic effect as unpaid actors and actresses, or that we are engaging ourselves in faithful *anamnesis,* faithfully reliving that common friendship which was sealed through the shedding of Christ's blood at Calvary. To turn the act of eucharist into make-believe is nothing short of turning blood into water. To share in the real presence of Christ at the Lord's table is to say to each other that blood is thicker than water, and to mean what we say. Not only does this relationship give us a new identity and ethic, it also opens for us new possibilities of freedom. We are set free from the captivity of our own ethnicity, middle-classness, social symbols, self-centeredness, and laws of self-preservation, so that we can dare to be friends with those who share a new covenant relationship with us.

Robert Neville of Boston University says this of humanity: "The covenantal character of the human condition is to have an actual state of affairs that is normed by ideals. We are created to be related to one another and to the rest of nature, and to the institutions connecting these, with righteousness, piety, faith, and hope."[60] What Neville says of the human being is particularly significant for the Christian. The irony is that Christians often use their freedom to become the friends of nature, dogs, cats, and trees, but find it impossible to become friends of each other. Can we covenant for friendship then, and take risks with each other, beyond just being friendly? We who are the dearly beloved of God, can we love one another for real? Can we become dynamically engaged in what C. S. Lewis called Appreciative Love, but what I prefer to call Affirmative Love? Can we dare to live differently in the church, even if we create an oasis of love in a desert of hatred? Can we confront the adversarial politics in our culture with a mutually affirmative spirituality in our church? What are some of the strategies we might adopt? Let us look briefly at some of them.

One: We can revisit the entire theological enterprise to see where it needs to be emancipated and made more user-friendly. To begin with, we theologians will need to stop taking ourselves and our importance so seriously, and invite others to do the same when they are around us. Why? Simply because we are trying to build systems around a God whom we have never seen. We should therefore be prepared to travel lightly. Faith is fun, and no one can either prove faith or disprove it. Why? Simply because we are beating the air in offering guidelines to people who have no intention of taking them seriously. There is no such thing as theological authority. This means that much of our sacred arrogance is misplaced. Why? Simply because we are merely artisans, trying out our craft in an organizational structure that is entirely voluntary. Nobody has to go to church, let alone obey the church. It is the principal job of the theologian to play the fool for Christ in tricking his disciples into becoming friends with one another, and in discovering creative and imaginative ways to make this happen.

Two: We must forge new ways of promoting a practical theology of ministry as friendship. How? By not only declericalizing the laity, but also by "decollarizing" the clergy. In God's new family household, neither ordination nor non-ordination means anything, but only the new creature; and as many as live by this rule, may peace be on them and on the whole household of God. How? By making sure that every ordination we hold is not the elevation of one who has squeezed through the net. It is rather the creation of another living symbol of what the communion of friends is all about, and the enlistment of another enabler of friendships within the Body of Christ. We must ordain lively friend-makers for the ministry of Christ.

How is this accomplished? By helping our ministers to deal effectively with their loneliness. Generally speaking, the minister is an administrator, a preacher, a social commentator, a priest, an evangelist, an educator, a spiritual leader, a budding psychiatrist, a political activist, a social welfare worker, a chauffeur, a director of community programs, a scholar, a cultic figure, a role model, an imaginary parent or spouse, an agent of compassionate gullibility, a possessor of supernatural powers, among other things. And yet the minister often suffers from loneliness. As ordained ministers, we know how to minister to others, but we often fall short in looking after ourselves, or of allowing others to look after us. We urgently need a common spirituality of ministry that does not make any allowances for loners, or for persons addicted to loneliness. Ministry is always to be an experience of shared friendship. Ministers need to minister to each other, and our congregations must do all in their power to make sure that this happens. For to minister to the minister is just as important as being ministered to by the minister. If only we could come to see the whole church as the minister, then we would readily redefine ourselves as *partakers* in, rather than as *possessors of*, the ministry to which we are called.

Three: We need to rebuild our seminaries, the places where we engage in the formation of Christian leadership, and service the vision of our churches. The life of the seminary must resemble that of a super-home, and not that of a supermarket. If we train men and women to shop around for ordination packages, we will only end up producing hustlers as ministers. The Christian vocation is a vocation into friendship, and the seminary has to be the place par excellence, where genuine human friendship is explored, practiced, cultivated, and made available to the rest of the church. So the quality of the common life together, the *koinonia,* is critically important; the letter grades are not all that important. The fertile and dynamic interaction between instructor and student, between student and student, is important in classroom, hallway, refectory, living room, chapel, or playing field. Seminary life is perhaps the most conspicuous barometer we have of telling what the friendship-level in the wider church is known, or expected, to be. It is chiefly through the seminary that we get an instant reading of the church's blood count.

Four: What do we do on Sunday mornings? So much of the parish budget is spent on the Sunday morning event—bulletins, music, sermons, heating, buildings, food, programs—and yet, most of the week bears little resemblance to that very expensive event. It is as if we invest our money to keep Sunday morning away from the rest of our lives. What a callous waste of scarce resources! How can our liturgies become less like staged dramatic events with masks and costumes, and more effective of live encounters of friendships in the making? How can we create imaginative symbols of friendship and mutual affirmation in our common worship, especially where there is the flexibility to do so? How can we turn "church" into a "worshiping community," so that those who do it together feel increasingly awkward in doing it by themselves? Can our liturgies really inspire and empower us to love one another as the dearly beloved? If not, why not?

●

In conclusion, we must patiently accept the fact that even if we cannot change the world, we can at least make an effort to change ourselves through the grace of God. As Christians, we are all called to ministry, and the call to ordination itself is neither a higher nor a lower call, it is only a call within a call. Our common call to ministry must be pursued in terms of service, faithfully and with endearment. For us, ministry means discipleship; ministry means servanting; ministry also means friendship—for the One who calls us also calls us friends. Someone has said that friendship is that "mutual harmony in affairs human and divine coupled with benevolence and charity." Anders says that "friendship is a matter of eternity, a taste of timelessness that we can only imagine as our destiny and a unity beyond what any of us have known to this point. When it is friendship in Christ, there is that dimension of concern for the spiritual good of the other and your own part in it—not in control, but in caretaking of the gift between you."[61] I believe that all this becomes truly enriching for us all when we take seriously the challenge of loving one another for God's sake.

Our friends are those whom God has made in God's own image. They exist everywhere—certainly beyond the boundaries of family, church, culture, and race. Those who are specially loved by God are those who have hardly anyone to call their own. They are the poor, the marginalized, the dispossessed, the hopeless ones. God is unconditionally on their side. Loving them for God's sake is a central imperative of our Christian vocation. Becoming engaged in their full human development is not simply an optional extra, but an integral part of the ministry of discipleship, friendship, service, and partnership, to which all Christians are called. Some are specially called by God to take the lead in ministering to these tender sheep of God. We often call such people pastors. They are God's servants, set apart for special functions in God's community of faithful sheep. In the next chapter, therefore, we will turn to a theological reflection of what such functions might entail, and to an exploration of the possible challenges involved in a life of pastorly vocation.

CHAPTER SIX

POWERFUL
SERVANTS OF
SERVANTS

"THIS IS HOW ONE SHOULD REGARD US, AS SERVANTS of Christ and stewards of the mysteries of God" (1 Cor 4:1). Paul uses these words to establish a very pivotal principle of what he understands to be the basic character of his ministry. He takes no credit himself for the ministry, and he does not understand why anyone should be boasting. After all, Paul asks, "What have you that you did not receive? If then you received it, why do you boast as if it were not a gift?" (1 Cor 4:7). The time for evaluation and assessment has not finally come, says Paul. In any case, it is not a matter for any human court to determine; that will be a matter for the Lord, when the Lord comes.

Does his ministry have a model? No, for it is always unfolding, and models hardly allow for any unfolding. Does his ministry have a purpose? Yes, it is the preaching of Christ as the Realm of God. Does his ministry have a mandate? Yes, it is "required of stewards that they be found trustworthy." Paul's apostolate lacked both institutions and ordination, but it certainly did not lack for critics. He was far too busy to take his critics seriously. Actually he said, "I do not even judge myself." The critical factor, he said, was that every person receive his or her own commendation from God. That was enough for him. For even if he may have been a fool for Christ, he still knew himself to be an imitator of Christ.

Is Paul's understanding of his apostolate radically different from our contemporary understanding of ministry? What did he want out of his ministry that we do not want out of ours? How does his task distance him from our understanding of ours today? He was a missionary; so are we. He had his critics; none of us lacks them. He speaks about ministry in terms of servanthood, stewardship, mysteries of God, gift, trustworthiness, Christlikeness, outsiderness, paying the price (not getting paid), waiting for the final verdict of God. How does our language about our own ministry measure up to his? How do we seek to project our own ministry? What do we mean when we call ourselves God's ministers of Christ, whether we are ordained or not? How does such a claim work itself out today in a world that is vastly different from the world of Saul of Tarsus? Several factors suggest themselves.

One: As baptized Christians, we are all followers of one about whom we know so little, but yet one in whom we resolutely claim to live, and move, and have our being. In terms of ministry, the problem for us is that Jesus himself was not a minister. He even bypassed ministerial duties like baptizing, or burying, or marrying, or paying the bills (Judas Iscariot did that!). He had no bishop, no church boards, no annual church budgets to raise. He just walked about homeless, hungry, harassing, and being harassed. It was his religious harassment of the Jewish power structure that eventually led to his death. So Jesus was Jesus, unique and special. Finding himself unable to forget the image of Isaiah's Suffering Servant, he does a little *preaching* here and there, a little *teaching*, with a touch of *healing* now and again. Peter summarizes Jesus' ministry in this way: "God anointed Jesus of Nazareth with the Holy Spirit and with power;...he went about doing good and healing all who were oppressed by the devil, for God was with him. We are witnesses to all that he did..." (Acts 10:38–39). But there was certainly no ritual, no liturgies to speak of, for he annoyed the people in his hometown church. None of this activity lasted long, for in three short years it was all over. When we say that we are representing Christ, what are we really representing, since he left us so little to go on?

Two: Our claims about Jesus are different from the claims that Jesus makes about himself. He does not claim to be the Christ, nor does he request any of his followers to make such a claim. He only speaks of God as his Father, and spends his time preaching about the in-breaking of the Realm of God. But the totality of his life and death makes such an indelible impact on the consciousness of his closest followers that Peter thunders forth on the Day of Pentecost: "Let all the house of Israel know assuredly that God has made him both Lord and Christ, this Jesus whom you crucified" (Acts 2:36). Paul puts the same claim another way: "designated to be Son of God in power according to the Spirit of holiness by his resurrection from the dead, Jesus Christ our Lord..." (Rom 1:4).

So Jesus preaches the Realm of God, and his followers preach Jesus as the Realm of God, and they call him by the same name that is reserved for God. Jesus becomes known as Christ, and is worshiped as Lord. It therefore looks as if we cannot claim to be *ministers of Christ* without taking on the added burden of being *servants of the Realm of God*. God's ministers of Christ and the servants of the Realm of God are one and the same people. This sometimes causes some problems when questions about institutions and ordination get in the way of what the unordained Jesus seemed to be about, or what the non-institutional Realm of God seems to demand. For Jesus says that the Realm of God is within us, beyond the reach of institutions. But we often seem to need our institutions. We cannot get very far without them.

Three: In an attempt to be all things to all people, ordained ministers very often experience what is commonly called "burnout." Those who study the careers of professionals tell us that such conditions begin long in advance with the initial burst of naive enthusiasm. Such enthusiasm is followed by experiences of stagnation, followed by feelings of extreme frustration, and finally apathy, burnout, and perhaps even some forms of moral, physical and spiritual breakdown. Ministers are clearly not immune to such a scenario; and we need to ask ourselves seriously, what the conditions are that we wittingly or unwittingly create to make such unwholesome occurrences inevitable. Ministers are not gods, and there should not be any attempt to encourage god-play in the church, or even in the wider society. We are only God's ministers, servants of Christ, and there can surely be some working acknowledgment that our natural human limitations are products of the divine creative wisdom, rather than the offshoot of some primordial catastrophic mistake.

Four: We also need to look at the role of religion itself, especially in a culture of religious freedom, religious pluralism, and what is now called civil religion. It has sometimes been said that nothing so masks the face of God as religion itself. When this is so, it places the ministry of the church under grave moral strain. We must not forget the words of the late James Hopewell, in which he warned against religion becoming the opium of ministry. Hopewell wrote:

> Far more prevalent than magic...has been the seduction for us to engage in religion. Religion is that pos-

sibility of dealing with the beliefs and behaviors of faithful people without being personally claimed in the faith they express. Religion is the illusion that grace and human response are an objective reality without subjective consequences. Religion for the minister is the commodity that can be concocted, the system that can be analyzed, the condition that—if one is skillful—can be delivered in teaching, worship, and pastoring. How devilish the tempter is! By making us feel that we are purveyors of religion he leads us away from personal faith into any number of works that supposedly deal with another's religion....[62]

Hopewell brings before our notice that critical difference between being a minister of religion and a person of faith, and reminds us they are not always synonymous.

How shall we serve when the reason for serving is so unclear, or confusing? In spite of this however, we dare not be unmindful of the fact that it is God, and God alone, who calls this community into being. It is God's *ecclesia,* called together for a specific purpose, and formed by a divine character, however much our historical limitations may happen to blur that character. The church, as God's community, is the evangelical community, the community shaped by the gospel, the community of forgiveness, the community responsive to God's call to mission, the community of those who are being set free—the emancipated and emancipatory community, the community of anticipation. This anticipatory community now enjoys a foretaste of that for which it actively and passionately waits. I mean the fullness of God's glorious Realm. Christian ministry may be confused from time to time, but it has no other source from which to draw its character or its nurture. We have only to learn how to grapple with the truth of having this heavenly treasure in earthen vessels and, as Christians, whether ordained or not, we must be eternally vigilant about how we take hold of sacred things with clumsy hands.

Five: In the light of all that we have just said, we still need to recognize that we as a church do not exist in a vacuum, nor does the church's ministry take place in a vacuum. The church is still a community among communities. But far more significantly, the church, through its members, encompasses many communities at the same time. How do we cope with this fact? For example, think how many actual social groupings, classes, movements, and neighborhoods are represented in any large congregation on a Sunday morning. Do we leave all our connections behind when we come together as church? The answer is resoundingly *no*. It is this which creates the greatest paradox of all, for it is at once a human problem as well as a divine possibility. God can cope with it in the church, but alas, we often cannot.

Robert Bellah and his colleagues, in their book, *The Good Society,* refer to this reality in terms of "the public church." They speak about our multiple loyalties, and contend that our religious loyalty transcends our national loyalty. They speak about the generosity in the giving of our time and money, greater than among any other group in the country. But they also speak about the tensions that exist between local congregations and para-church organizations, and also about the powerful institutions in the country which influence our lives and absorb so much of our energies. They describe these as seeming "to pressure us to compete for individual advantage rather than to combine for the common welfare, and they empty out meaning from our lives when they structure our existence as a competitive race for money, power, prestige, or the consumer goods that symbolize them."[63]

The question is how do you do ministry in a public church that is riddled with privatized and competitive religion? How do we come to understand ourselves as God's ministers of Christ in such a context, when so much of what we take for granted runs counter to all that Jesus of Nazareth lived and died for? If we are to be the servants of the One who was totally and unconditionally open toward others, how do we minister to those who seem to be totally and unconditionally concerned only about themselves, and further threaten to withhold their donations when we seek to point them to Christ? How do we set priorities for ministry in the face of such a dilemma?

Servants of the Chief—But Which One?

It seems to me that we can begin to confront this major difficulty by acknowledging the fact that the public church is also the community of charisms, the community of gifts, the charismatic community. As public and as complex as it is, it is still the community of the Spirit. This is not just *your* private spirit, or *my* competitive spirit, but more importantly the Spirit of God. As many as are prepared to be led by the Spirit of God, they remain, and continue to become, children of God. The Spirit of God bestows gifts on whomever the Spirit wills, and spiritual gifts become practical gifts, for they are used preeminently in the proclamation of the gospel, and in the practice of our living faith in Jesus as Lord and Christ.

This is precisely what it means to be God's ministers of Christ. This is precisely what it means to confess our faith in God as Creator, Redeemer, and Sustainer. There can be no confession of faith in this way that excludes confession of faith in God's church. Those who believe in God also believe in God's church—and that is precisely why we do ministry. The marks of the Church—unity, holiness, catholicity, and apostolicity—to which we have continually

referred throughout this book, not only draw their sub-
stance from the life of the church in the New Testament,
but they also create for us four distinct marks of ministry
to which we now turn our attention. These four marks of
ministry are: sacrament, stewardship, servanthood, sign.
We will take each of them in turn.

First, when we speak of the unity of the church as one
of its four marks, we are drawing on our primary understanding of the oneness of God, the single and unrepeatable nature of God's calling the church into being, as well
as on our estimate of the church as the Body of Christ. The
mark of ministry that follows from this is that of **sacrament**. The Christian ministry is a sacramental gift from
God to each of us, and in that gift there is God's own self-
giving. Our ministry then is an outward and visible manifestation of an inward and spiritual relationship, freely
initiated by God, sustained through the indwelling of
God's Spirit, and making us ever ready to bring forth the
fruit of good works.

The sacramentality of the ministry is not just proclaimed in ordination, it actually begins with our baptism, and we are called to a level of spiritual response that
is always in keeping with our capacity to respond. For to
whom much is given, of them shall much always be
required. There is no time out. To live out the sacramental
nature of our ministry, however, is not to adopt a holier-
than-thou attitude to anyone, but rather to struggle for
the emergence of a spirituality that is communal, open to
God's many surprises in the world, liberative, and capable
of drawing ourselves and others closer to the throne of
God's grace. Ministry that is sacramental and deeply spiritual can never fail to be effective as a living vessel of
God's lovely grace. Above all, it means that we will always
strive to be gracious with everyone for whom Christ died.

There are some implications that follow from this

understanding of ministry as sacrament. First, not only do we share in the sacramental community of the Body of Christ, but we also share who we are, and what we believe, both within and without that Body.

Another major implication has to do with evangelism. It is always important to make the distinction between evangelicalism, evangelization, and evangelism. *Evangelicalism* is a brand of Christian belief and practice which places primary emphasis on the Word of God. It flourishes in many branches of the Christian church. *Evangelization* is that concentrated missionary activity of preaching the gospel on the frontiers of other cultures and faiths with a view to radical conversion and change of lifestyle. *Evangelism* is really a sharing of one's faith, and every Christian is expected to be an evangelist, for it is really a third-order activity. First you believe it, next you try it, then you share it. But you cannot honestly share what you are not trying for yourself. The ministry as sacrament requires that we share ourselves and our faith unconditionally with others, just as God in Jesus has shared the divine love unconditionally with us. Ministry is the sacramental life of sharing.

Second, we look at the holiness of the church. The church as God's household is the Holy Church, and the mark of ministry here is that of **stewardship**. The minister of Christ is God's steward in God's household. Stewardship involves trust, and commitment, and accountability to the One from whom the trust has been derived, and the readiness to understand and accept the limitations of the trust, and the undying need to be trustworthy.

Ministry as stewardship will always involve a constant updating of the catalog of gifts with which one has been entrusted. Sometimes the nature of the gifts changes. Sometimes they are withdrawn without our notice, and we are reluctant to admit it. It must always remain true that the Lord who gives is also the Lord who takes away.

Ministry grows and changes, just as our lives evolve in a variety of ways. The nature of the minister as steward is powerfully contained in some words which the late Abraham Heschel used to describe his friend Reinhold Niebuhr's spirituality as one which combined heaven and earth, not separating soul from body, or worship from living. We can learn from Heschel's words that although the minister is also to administer, although stewardship involves management and administration, it also involves integration—the integration of the gospel story with the human story, the integration of the sacred with the secular.

Third, we look at the catholicity of the church. We understand catholicity in terms of totality, and universality, and eternity. Yet we also understand it in terms of freedom, and openness, and classlessness, and the absence of preconditions, or prejudice, or arrogance. The catholic church is also the free church, and the free church is also the serving church. The mark of ministry therefore is that of **servanthood,** and it draws its distinction from the New Testament image of the church as the community of believers, or the people of God. Such a mark is informed by the words of Jesus in Mark 10:45: "The Son of Man came not to be served but to serve, and to give his life as a ransom for many."

This is the principal way in which we participate in the life of Christ and share in the imitation of Christ. We imitate Christ by serving others as Christ served, and by seeking to offer ourselves and our service in the cause of bringing in the Realm of God. So the servant ministry is not just about doing good works, it is also about being good persons for the sake of Christ and the salvation of the world. Who we are very often speaks more loudly than all that we do. For example, we need to be careful not to be so much involved in headcounts, and other forms of accounting, that we neglect to turn our members into disciples.

Jesus has sent us into the world to make disciples by feeding his sheep; he did not command us to attract members for the sake of counting them.

We have already paid a great deal of attention to the theme of servanthood in this book, especially in Chapter Four. Nevertheless, it is a theme which demands constant discussion in a book such as this which carries the title *Serving with Power*. For it is the power of serving God, and of serving God's world through the power of the gospel, which we believe can make an immeasurable difference in our human relationships. During the past decade several theologians have been contributing to the theological debate about the significance of servanthood for the ministry of Christians. I propose to refer here to some thoughts by Ronald Sunderland and James Cone.

Sunderland suggests that the church which seeks to move away from suffering, whether its own or that of the poor and the oppressed, is also moving away from its servanthood. It is renouncing the servanthood offered by Jesus. He gives two human reasons for this. First, we try to avoid pain wherever we can, and second, "we are tempted to reject a servanthood that compels us to take responsibility for our choices and embrace a bondage that is characterized by the *avoidance* of decision-making."[64] He goes on to suggest that Christians must allow servanthood to control all their decisions, and he speaks of it as being "all-encompassing in its reach and application." The character of servanthood, he says, "compels the servant to live as an exemplar of living service, and the community of servants as the first fruits of the society so created."[65] For, if that community's witness is to have integrity, it must conform to the character of servanthood "embodied by its Lord."

James Cone asserts that the belief in Christ as the Lord of the church acknowledges the church as the servant of

Christ. He warns against any undue spiritualizing of servanthood "so as to camouflage its concrete, political embodiment." This political dimension calls for active commitment to a struggle on the side of the poor and oppressed. Cone says: "Servanthood is the opposite of the world's definition of lordship."[66] Cone sees the church as a crucified community living under the cross, but he also sees the church as a vibrant community of hope: "It believes that the things that are can and ought to be otherwise." Quite naturally such a strong faith is only possible because, as Cone affirms, "God is the power who transforms the suffering of the present into the hope of the future."[67]

The fourth mark is that of apostolicity. The early church is known as the apostolic community, and is also referred to as *the Way* in the Acts of the Apostles. We have already discussed the significance of "the Way" in Chapter Three. Such a character of the church reminds us always of the constant movement taking place in the church. It is a band of people moving forward, moving outward, moving upward—for it is called away from itself to be fully involved in God's mission. Yet we have to remember that God's mission is not the only mission there is in the world. Many forces and groupings wish to claim the world for their own possession and dominance. There is always a battle going on for the soul of the world; not a battle between good and evil, but a battle between good and good. For what is good for us is not always identical with what is good for others. So we need signs, clearly distinguishing marks about who we are, what we are about, where we are heading, and what we have going for us. Ministry then is to be a living **Sign**. It is a sign of the Realm of God. It is a warning against evil. It is a concrete assurance that God is still around and very active. It is a challenge to come and join. It is a banner that says that we do have something to shout about. The ministry of the church is to be the most conspicuous sign that the church is seriously committed to what God has called it into being for, that the Realm of God is surely on the way, and that we are a guaranteed foretaste of what it is all about. To use the words of the First Letter of John, we are to become who we are already.

Ministry as a sign then is to be a transforming ministry; it must make a difference wherever it takes place, and always a difference for the better. Richard Bondi, in his book *Leading God's People* says: "Ministry must be transforming, and for that to happen we must be continually transforming ministry."[68] Bondi also says: "Continual transformation is required to keep the people of God moving toward the destination of their hearts. Transforming ministry in the leadership of that movement is a difficult and threatening enterprise in an uncertain world and in the face of such wide rifts in the Body of Christ. Yet taking up that leadership as a vocation and trusting in our ability in Christ to live it out is, as Paul would put it, another way of boasting not in humans but in the Lord."[69]

So, what's the point of trying to be God's ministers of Christ in such a sinful world as this? Is there any value in all this religious activity and concern? Is there any point in trying to be good, or in trying to serve God, or to minister for God's sake? Where does it get us? What do we take to the bank? How do we break through to those new challenges as God's ministers of Christ? These are questions which test us all as Christians at the very core of our beings. Paul would answer: "All that may be true, but it is required of God's ministers that they be found faithful." Jesus adds to that: "Be thou faithful unto death and I will give thee a crown of life." It should be our most fervent and earnest duty to let these four marks of ministry— sacrament, stewardship, servanthood, sign—help to strengthen our witness and, by the grace of God, increase our faith.

Robert N. Bellah and his colleagues offer us this useful thought:

> Members of biblical religions are under the obligation to listen to what God is saying in the most mundane events of everyday life as well as in the great events of world history, and to respond as conscientiously as they can to the ethical demands raised by those events. Yet it is easier to repeat old formulas, to comfort oneself with the community's familiar practices, than to risk trusting a new response to new conditions. Yet if we are fortunate enough to have the gift of faith through which we see ourselves as members of the universal community of all being, then we bear a special responsibility to bring whatever insights we have to the common discussion of new problems, not because we have any superior wisdom but because we can be....ambassadors of trust in a fearful world."[70]

God never asks for more. As ministers of Christ, we are also ambassadors of trust, and we should never be satisfied with less.

How then do bishops, or their counterparts, as chief servants of the church and as leading ministers in our churches, help the rest of us to cope with these critical issues of ministry which we have been addressing thus far?

Bishops as Chief Servants? Or Chiefs?

There can hardly be any doubt that the ecclesiological task, that is, the task of understanding the nature of the church and of faithfully exercising one's ministry within the church, is inherently circumscribed by a number of tensions and contradictions. These create innumerable difficulties for church leaders. Pressure points abound, and they engender not only a sense of gravity and compulsion, but also a consciousness of the meaning of authority, whether it is the authority of the church itself (however that is defined), or of one's exercise of personal authority within the church. The most fundamental of these pressure points, I would suggest, is the tension between leaving it to God and sending God on leave. Some theologians would call this a tension between a theistic faith and a deistic practice. That is the critical difference between actively believing that God is in control in the here and now, and that God has left it to us to "fix it" in God's name.

This carries with it all kinds of implications for divine forgiveness for the socially unforgivable. It means refusing to cast the stone at those whom we think deserve to be stoned; upholding the letter of the ecclesiastical or civil law, while preserving the spirit of love and compassion; maintaining the integrity of church order and discipline for the sake of the whole, while seeking to rescue the lost sheep for whom the Good Shepherd laid down his very life. These implications are based on the pressure points of our conflicting conceptions of ecclesiology, our understanding of what the church is truly to be about, and our fuzzy understanding of who God is, what God wants, how God works, and when we, as they say, "let go and let God." The occasional temptation is to let God go and to start playing God ourselves.

There is also the accompanying pressure point concerning the tension between official accountability and personal responsibility. Because the ecclesiological task is attended by the sense of continuity and tradition, those who are mainly charged with the oversight (*episcope*) of the community carry with them the burden of ensuring that things do not falter on their watch. And yet they are faced with the daily realities of changing contexts, the social and political demands of expediency, exceptional cases which demand extraordinary responses, and new patterns of human behavior and misbehavior, for which neither the traditions of the church, nor the manuals of discipline have adequately prepared or directed them.

Another important pressure point has to do with the complicated multicultural context in which the ecclesiological task has to be carried out today. America is nothing like first-century Palestine. How does one make the time leap of 1900 years and remain faithful to the original designs of the gospel? The New Testament gives us a *feel* for the church, but it does not come anywhere near to giving us a *form* for the church. How does the builder (bishop) in the church community function in the face of such a strong conflict between the contemporary social images of the church and its traditional images in the gospel? On the other hand, are there images that should be abandoned in the light of today's prevailing conditions? Such conditions include: a) the primacy of the individual over the community; b) the predominance of the principle of property over the person in our common law; c) the categorization of human beings into levels of power, based on race, ability, gender and ethnicity, over against the rights of people to be fully human. I consider that these create enormous conditions for pressure points in the ecclesiological task, for we bring our whole world with us into the community of faith, sometimes even in search of validation and affirmation for some of these trends. In other words, most of our ecclesial habits are influenced by our non-ecclesial circumstances.

In the final chapter of my recent book *Can God Save the*

Church? I offered a brief discussion on what I consider to be three basic evils in our contemporary social ethos, and four crucial issues for the common life of the church. I list the evils as unemployment, materialism, and pragmatism, and the issues as gender, sexuality, race and AIDS. The opening chapter of the book raised the question: Can the Church be saved? My answer was: Not on its own terms. I suggested that the tragedy of the present century is that the church has allowed itself to lapse into a false sense of assurance that it can both offer salvation and be emancipated on terms which it can negotiate. God's salvation, I pointed out, is God's alone, and no other source can dare claim prior rights or privilege (p. 10). I also suggested that the church will need to demonstrate prophetically that healing is possible in a broken world, chiefly by becoming more and more a healing and compassionate community. And that by offering to the world a new way of accepting God's reconciling grace, which is in effect to embrace the brokenness of God in Jesus, the fracturedness in postmodern society can be challenged (p. 11).

We are really faced with more than a question of world orientation versus otherworldliness. It is about our authentic response of faith to a world-making, world-saving, and world-affirming God, who not only called the church into being beyond the moribund chains of religion and ethical traditions, but who founded it on a new reality and a new ethic. That new reality was the resurrection of Jesus, who was supremely the historical embodiment of the new ethic of love. Thus the church as the new community of the resurrection was "sent back into the life of the world with a new exposure to its brokenness and a new concern for its mending," to use Bonhoeffer's words. Religion puts Jesus to death. Resurrection brings new life in Jesus. Peter Hodgson of Vanderbilt University says: "Religion provides a convenient escape for those who lack the strength to cope with the threats of modernity; it does not often enough provide resources for those who wish to respond to its challenges."[71] The tension between the law of religion and the new life of resurrection is perhaps the gravest of all pressure points in our ecclesiological task today. The challenge for bishops, clergy and people is always to ensure that the word *church* has more of the force of a verb than of a noun. Church is *what we do* and not just *who we are*.

Throughout the course of our discussion in this book we have looked at the church from a number of different angles, mainly with respect to the central concept of "community." I do not believe that we can go too far wrong if we stay close to that operative paradigm of community. Closely allied with this paradigm, however, has to be the biblical paradigm of "covenant." Basically we understand "covenant" as a right relationship with God. When we speak of the church as the community of the New Covenant, we find that this approach is replete with implications both for the ecclesiological task as well as for the meaning of our life together as co-workers with God through Christ.

It seems to me that the concept of New Covenant really begins with Jeremiah, where he places emphasis on the relationship with God in the heart, but is leading up to the resurrection of Jesus Christ. It has to do with forgiveness, but more particularly with freedom. It has to do with new life in the Spirit. It has to do with the unconditional freedom of God and the celebration of that freedom. Covenant means that God strikes a bargain of freedom with us. In my book *Can God Save the Church?* I say: "It is the nature of the Christian Gospel to demonstrate that faith in the God of Jesus is itself a divine gift of freedom, bound up with the Christ who belongs to God. Such is the freedom that creates anew and saves; it does not destroy.

The New Testament faith is that it emancipates the believer from the slavery of sin, the slavery of fear, the slavery of the threat of death, the slavery of the law of self-interests, and the slavery from the power of [complexes]" p. 25).

Not only is the church the community of covenantal freedom, it is also the community for the interpretation and appropriation of that freedom. The word of God, the will of God, and the work of God, in all of God's unconditional freedom, have to be mediated to the world and appropriated in the conduct of the community of faith. This means that authoritative texts in the community require authoritative interpreters, and authoritative interpreters are required to take the lead in the appropriate embodiment of their meaning and significance. Bishops therefore enjoy no grounds for exemption in this regard.

Covenantal ecclesiology goes further to suggest that the community of the New Covenant is also the fellowship of the Spirit, the communion of the Spirit. The communion of the Spirit is a community of persons, a differentiated community that is guided by love as the power of its unity, and enlightened by freedom as the power of its diversity. Within such a community there is not an enforced uniformity, but rather a growth in communicative relationships, continuing to set its members free. Communicative relationships inevitably bring conflicts, but they also engender a mutuality of support for each other's sense of freedom toward God. The communion of the Spirit is a community of sharing, a community for creative and responsive faith in which persons do not have to be refashioned in each other's image.

Covenantal ecclesiology also suggests a community of trust through a fellowship in the Spirit, for covenants require trust and assume trustworthiness at the same time. Just as we are required within the church to trust in the trustworthiness of God, we are also expected through the risky nature of our faith to trust each other for God's sake. Jurgen Moltmann speaks of trust in this way:

> Trust is the art of living not only in what we have in common, but in our differences as well—not merely with people like ourselves but with others too. If in the Christian community common trust springs from the love of Christ, and if it is the fellowship of the Spirit which brings together people who are different, that fellowship will become the source which strengthens our capacity for community in the natural relationships of life.[72]

The church as the fellowship of the Spirit has to thrive on two very critical factors—conflicting ecclesiologies and fragmented ecclesial memories. These are living realities in the life of the church. On the one hand there are often variations on the theme of what is the most appropriate way of being the church in any given social, historical, cultural or geographical context. Political realities and constituent predilections often define the flavor of ecclesiology in different ecclesiastical districts, or even within those districts. Where a church denomination is largely comprised of a membership of persons who have come from other denominational persuasions, these persons bring with them many things. They bring most of their ecclesial habits and expectations, their sense of search and pilgrimage, their varieties of tastes and styles of religious behavior, and their competing vested interests. They also bring their own ideological commitments for a particular form of church involvement. In such cases, the living memory of that church must of necessity be a fragmented reality. All of this must be accepted as a divine blessing, and not just as a mixed blessing, however difficult and complex it might first appear to be. The plurality of ecclesiologies and ecclesial memories must lead us into an experience of authentic community, guided by the Spirit, rather than imprison us within the chains of our own religious prejudice.

The church as the covenantal community then, as the fellowship of the Spirit, is the sphere in which people seek and experience the nearness of Jesus as they continue their relentless search for transcendence, for personal meaning in their lives, and for nurturing community. Bishops take the lead in helping to create the atmosphere for such a search. At the center of it all is the search for truth, for the church's proclamation, according to the Fathers of the church, is always to be understood as the "rule of truth." But it is always a truth in dialogue with the world, in order that it may come to a more profound understanding of the truth that it proclaims. Walter Kasper reminds us that truth is not divisive in character. He says: "Truth without love becomes chauvinistic, intolerant and totalitarian. But love without truth is blind and dumb, and beneath the dignity of human beings. It pretends common ground outwardly which does not inwardly exist."[73] Kasper goes on to speak of an inner solidarity that has to exist between truth and love which is: "the profoundest reason why the fellowship of the church is the place of truth. And just because it is the place of truth, the church is a prophetic sign and instrument of unity, peace and reconciliation in the world."[74] Covenantal ecclesiology therefore demands of us that we acknowledge the church as the place of truth, that living and lively community that is led by the Spirit of truth. It is the same Spirit who is promised to guide us into all truth, and who makes it possible for us to experience God's sanctifying, transforming and liberating effects in our common life together. I therefore agree with Peter Hodgson who says that: "The church must become in praxis what it understands itself to be in essence, and often it only discovers in praxis what it ought to be in essence."[75]

The writer of the First Letter to Timothy speaks of the office and work of the bishop as a noble task. This is very much in keeping with the concepts of the ecclesiological task that we have just been discussing. The nobility of the bishop's job comes not from the social status which it confers, nor from the right to be dressed in purple and fine linen, but rather from the fact that it is central to the ongoing life, edification and welfare of the church for which the Christ of God gave his life. The ecclesiological task is essentially a lived-out participation in the extension of Christ's incarnation. Nobility is conferred on it by God, not by the society. Because of this, the bishop is called to be above reproach, monogamous, temperate, sensible, respectable, hospitable, an apt teacher, sober, non-violent, gentle, not cantankerous and quarrelsome, and absolutely non-venal ("not a lover of money"). The bishop must be able to demonstrate sound leadership ability with respect to family matters, since these traits will serve as an indicator for the leadership and administration of the household of God. Additionally, the bishop should not be a newcomer (novice) to the fold, since this would almost certainly be indicative of that person's movement on an ego-trip, a fast track to career development, or worse still, that person's zeal for the fulfillment of sheer ambition. The job description ends with these words: "Moreover, he must be well thought of by outsiders, so that he may not fall into disgrace and the snare of the devil" (1 Tm 3:7).

Over the centuries, various job descriptions of the office and work of bishops and church leaders have tended to reflect more the predilections of the communities, over which bishops are to be placed, as a sort of demographic projection rather than the working out of these ideals to which this New Testament outline would direct us. Consequently, the history of our churches has not always been blessed with the memories of a pilgrim people struggling to transcend the limitations and imperfections of our own social and cultural contexts and desires. In a real sense, it has been often true to say that, with our choice of bishops and other church leaders, we get what we pray for. But not even this bind should cause us to be unmindful of the fact that the bishop or other church leader, as chief servant in the community, is primarily answerable to God, of whose household we are. The basic job description consists in that faithful and obedient service to the One by whom the whole church is constantly called into being.

Bishops and other leaders of the church must therefore see themselves as being called to a higher, stronger, richer, and healthier witness of a practical covenantal ecclesiology through which they can guide the faithful people committed to their charge in the ways of justice and truth, of courage and righteousness, of faithfulness and peace. For just as we have been often referring to the *marks of the church,* so too we must now seek to identify the *marks of the bishop,* who is chief servant of the Servant, rather than chief of the servants. The life and witness of the bishop, or other church leader of leaders, must inevitably involve four visible and distinct marks as the marks of Christ. They are not far removed from what Paul speaks of as the marks of Jesus that he bears in his own body. "From now on," he says, "let no one make trouble for me; for I carry the marks of Jesus, branded on my body" (Gal 6:17).

I suggest that there are four such visible marks of the bishop who is called to be chief servant of the Servant. They are *discipleship, suffering, compassion, and sacrifice.* Allow me a brief word on each of these.

Discipleship—This is the state of becoming in which the follower of Jesus participates, led and empowered by the

Spirit of Christ. It is the existential Yes to the call of Jesus—
"Follow me." It is the fundamental character of Christian
existence, as well as the only measure of success in the
work of the apostolic community. We are sent out to make
disciples; we are not sent out to register members, and
then cultivate them into organizational submission.

Suffering—This is the inevitable consequence of Christian
discipleship, for the call to discipleship is the call to obedience to Christ, and that call always brings suffering. He
speaks of suffering as bearing the cross, not wearing it, of
drinking the cup, not serving it. Christian discipleship does
not have the option of destroying the cruciality of the cross,
because it is endowed with the grace by which that cross of
suffering can, in God's immediate or extended time,
become redemptive. Every aspect of suffering, even theological suffering at the hands of those with whom we vio-
lently disagree, can become redemptive, provided that we
do not rush to action like the sons of Boanerges, but suffer
patiently for what we consider to be the sake of the truth.
The church as the suffering community is also the community of grace—where grace and truth meet together, and
righteousness and peace kiss. In any event, we never suffer
alone. God suffers too.

Compassion—This follows naturally from the mark of
suffering, for only those who know what suffering is truly
know what it means to suffer with others. The whole
Christian story is based on an act of divine compassion,
without which the very essence of our spiritual lives would
be nullified. Compassion takes its form from our understanding of the nature of a God who, although understood
to be Ultimate Reality, still becomes known to us, and
among us, as Intimate Reality. Thus we are never exempt
from the hard task of sharing one another's burdens if we
are to be serious about fulfilling the law of Christ. Neither

God's justice, nor God's compassion, should ever be treated by bishops as if they were soft options.

Sacrifice—This is the central meaning and intention of all that we do as church, as we make present in our bodily existence a living sacrifice that is holy and worthy of divine acceptance. It takes its mandate from the cross. It provides us with our daily *anamnesis,* our active and concrete re-living of the sacrifice of Jesus, and our mission task of sharing, serving, and offering up that which is most precious for the saving work of God in Christ. Our practical ecclesiology then is incurably sacrificial, not because we demand it of others, but because we participate in it ourselves unconditionally, and with singleness of mind. Thus we are able to demonstrate that the church which lives in us, and we in it, is not only the fruit of God's salvation, wrought by a supreme act of sacrifice once for all, but is also the agent of that salvation. Our eucharistic vitality makes no sense except through the meaning of our sacrificial mentality.

All of these visible marks of the servant ministry are expected to be embodied, symbolized, and given concrete expression in the life and ministry of our bishops. Our bishops are our chief pastors, our shepherds in the community of Christ. They are expected to know their sheep and serve them, to lead their sheep and feed them, to direct their sheep and guard them, to seek their sheep and bring them back. They are the personalized centers of the church. They speak for, in, and to the church, more as its representatives than as individual members. As chief pastors, bishops are also chief servants who make a daily surrender of their individuality for the sake of the whole community of faith. The chief pastors are also the headwaiters—the *episcopoi* are the headwaiters over the *diakonoi,* the waiters. Not only are they to continue serving tables, they are also to see that all tables are served.

Bishops are called by God to do what the twelve Apostles found difficult. The Twelve said that they could not evangelize and serve tables at the same time. Bishops have no such luxury, for in their sacred office all duties and obligations of the apostolic ministry converge.

The office and work of a bishop, therefore, cannot be considered an easy task, nor can it ever be considered a mark of promotion. It is a specific vocation to which God, in his wisdom does not call all of us. It touches different people differently; all are not afforded the gifts from above to live out the five basic and foundational characteristics of the bishop's life that I call the five C's: *call, commitment, competence, character, collegiality.* It is this fifth characteristic of collegiality that sometimes poses difficulties for persons who serve at the top of their constituency, and who recognize that not only does the "buck stop here," but also that the "buck starts here."

The covenantal ecclesiology to which we must be committed cannot thrive without a massive surge of genuine collegial friendship among bishops and leaders in their various denominations. I am referring to a quality of friendship which combines affection with respect, faithfulness with freedom, and persistence with openness. The rest of the church will always take their cue from the leadership of the bishops in this regard, and not the other way around. All ecclesiologies in the end are based on the examples and styles which radiate from the center, and from the changes which often evolve therefrom. But at the root of it all lies the unamended rule that we should love one another as Christ has loved us. "The basic law of the community of Christ," says Moltmann, "is acceptance of others in their difference, for it is this experience of our neighbors, and only this, which is in line with Christian experience of God."[76]

●

In conclusion, as we seek to discover the true meaning of ministry, and as we struggle with what it means to be powerful servants of the servants of God, we do well to bear in mind that, as faithful Christians, we are all in this search for meaning and this struggle for wholeness together. Whether as signs, or stewards, or servants, or simply as Christians who carry neither labels nor titles, the central fact of our existence is that together we depend on the grace of God for that which we are and for that which we are to become. This requires of us a persistent openness to the leading and urgings of God's good Spirit. These urgings often take us down the paths of a new and surprising spirituality as we discern fresh ways of expressing the age-old faith once delivered to the saints. It is to a discussion of these fresh paths of spirituality for ministry, whether lay or ordained, particularly as it relates to the practice of the presence of God in our modern world, that we will now turn in the next chapter.

CHAPTER SEVEN

SPIRITUALITY
AND CULTURE

"**L**IFE IS LIKE A BOX OF CHOCOLATES," SAID FORREST Gump. "You never know what you're going to get." His mother told him so, he said. When these words were spoken in the film, *Forrest Gump,* they became an instant hit. So many people were overheard quoting them that they obviously indicated a level of social validity or authenticity which our Hollywood culture had not been able to produce for quite a long time. In many ways, it is the function of the movies, or television, or the stage, to return the society to itself, so that when the society hears echoes of itself, or sees its true image re-presented to it, there is always likely to be that instant recognition. Forrest Gump obviously achieved that. But what else is there that tells us about life as it most truly is? Is life nothing but a box of surprises? How do we work our way through its many and varied configurations and its incessant twists and turns? What do we make of the broad and often complex picture of life in our contemporary pluralistic culture?

In Chapter One we began by looking at some of the moral crises we have been facing in this society in more recent times. In Chapter Five it was pointed out that there is a sense in which America must always have an enemy, in order to be America. Swords and guns are inexorably more definitive of who we are than plowshares and harvesters. We were invited by President William Clinton in his 1997 State of the Union Address to consider "inaction" as America's chief enemy today. Only time will tell how America will wage war on such an enemy, and what the most effective weapons will be that we will use to fight, and who will become the sub-enemies in that war. We are perpetually surrounded by the culture of sin and the culture of the marketplace. The combination of these cultures produces social divisiveness and aggressive materialism, as it challenges America to take diversity into its system. Diversity of wealth and access, of origin and outlook, of memory and moment, of class and style, is seen by some as weakness, and by others as strength. For corporate America, "diversity training" is dead on arrival, in spite of the fact that more money is being spent on making provisions for such programs.

The *Newsweek* columnist Jack Kroll has offered us this comment: "As America inexorably moves toward a multifarious conflation of racial, ethnic and cultural identities, the task of creating a new synthesis becomes more difficult, and more crucial....This country had better learn to treat its differences as a source of fruition rather than hostility."[77] Perhaps no other issue has so exacerbated the fundamental differences at work in the American social psyche today as the outcome of the legal sagas of O.J. Simpson. To the extent that the Simpson trials have been interpreted by most of us as a powerful metaphor of what America is all about, we have certainly opted for treating diversity as a source of hostility, rather than as a gift of strength. It cannot be right for us to assume that differences in culture should necessarily become the groundwork for the cultivation of a culture of difference.

The Challenge of Human Experience

Throughout the course of the twentieth century, perhaps no other groups of people have suffered more from the culture of difference as have the people of African or Jewish descent. Recent disclosures have brought to our notice a quotation from the late mother of a very prominent American citizen: "To be a Jew is to be constantly threatened by some kind of danger. That is our history."[78] This is assumed to be the reason why certain information about their family history was perhaps left undisclosed for the sake of her children's well-being. In commenting on this struggle of "memory over forgetting," the journalist Michael Dobbs has offered these insights: "The historical amnesia that afflicts some first generation Americans is an entirely different kind of forgetfulness. It is a personal choice, a kind of survival instinct, not something that has been imposed from outside, by the state. The very act of emigrating to America can be, in many cases, a conscious decision to escape the past and start a new life. As a result, there are millions of Americans who know very little about what happened to their families prior to arriving in America."[79]

While this may well be true for the process of assimilation of most Jews into American society, the same cannot be said for the assimilation of persons of African descent. For us whom God has blessed with ebony grace—black people—the struggle is rather one of "forgetting over memory." America never lets us forget that we are black. Our inner determination to fight against all systems of marginalization, exclusion, and injustice keeps before our memory the need to overcome, if only for the sake of our ancestors on whose beaten backs we have been carried, and on whose weary shoulders we are proud to stand and determined to struggle. For while it has not always been easy, Jews have been able to overcome the barriers of ethnic differences because of their pigmentation. On the other hand, the prospect of blacks being fully accepted into the mainstream of public life and social leadership at the highest levels is apparently unattainable. For blacks, the culture of difference is inextricably bound up with the culture of inferiority, and eminent exceptions among black folk only serve to prove that rule.

In his very resourceful book, *Conversations With God,* the late Professor James Washington has shared with us some prayers of African Americans over the past two centuries. One such prayer is that composed by William Donnel Watley in 1992, which reads in part:

> O God, I get tired of racism wherever I go—abroad and at home. From stores that let me know that I have gotten "out of place"; from looks of fear that my black manly presence engenders in some; from small insults to major offenses; from polite, subtle, condescending paternalism or maternalism to outright, open hostility; from insulting jokes about my intelligence to curiosity about alleged black sexual prowess; from caricatures and stereotypes to the "you are the exception" syndrome—racism rears its many heads and shows its various faces all the time.[80]

The foregoing quotation speaks for itself about the difficulties in being black in America. One wonders how often during the course of each day some such prayer is offered up to God out of the crucible of one's blackness. The prayer should serve as a fitting reminder that, if to be a Jew is to be constantly faced with danger, then to be black is to be constantly open to suffering simply on the grounds of being black. To be black is to suffer for it. Ethnocentrism, therefore, when combined with racism and aggressive materialism, threatens the very meaning of human life itself and renders hazardous the prospects of achieving that fullness of life which was promised to all of us in Jesus as the Christ of God, the Savior and Emancipator of the world. This is precisely the context in which we are faced with the challenge of discovering a new spirituality for ministry which will meet the agonizing demands of human need at their deepest level. But what are the contours of human need, and how does any form of spirituality help to shape an effective ministry?

In general terms, it would perhaps be true to say that human life today is conditioned by a set of needs which extend well beyond the normal realm of religious concerns. Indeed, it might even be more correct to say that our religious concerns emerge out of the strains experienced by our struggles to meet our basic human needs— food, clothing, shelter, education, pure water, social access, civic equity, health care and recreation. Thus, when we seek to understand the pressures of life in our contemporary context, we are best aided in such a quest by a fresh look at what we most zealously strive for in our yearnings to be satisfied. Here is where we seem to be on common ground with most right thinking people, regardless of their personal religious persuasion. In the final analysis, we are basically human before we are religious. These common human needs may well be grouped into four categories.

First, we stand constantly in need of *self-recognition*. This means that we are never satisfied unless there is an acceptable level of knowing who we are, as well as being known by others. Some people refer to this as a search for self-identity; but this does not seem to me to be as deep as the need for self-recognition. We are all aware of people who pass through phases in their lives, not least, of course, our very selves. They move from one form of identity to another. Such phases are often dictated or delineated by a number of circumstances, be they emotional, relational, economic, social, ideological, spiritual, or even chronological. Times change, and so do men and women. But that sense of who they are, and not just how they would prefer to be identified, has an ongoing continuity from which there is no escape. For example, Jewish immigrants to America have been known to change their names, for reasons best known to themselves. Persons of African descent in America have sometimes been known to adopt African names in their adult years in order to make a statement about themselves and their outlook, with special focus against a European historical connection.

Such changes in names, or in appearance, may serve to satisfy the identity project, but they do not affect the self-recognition project. Changes of names do not necessarily affect our unfolding story, our memory, our limitations, our expectations, our sense of discipline and control, our sense of failure or success. We are still faced with our need to accomplish our dreams of one kind or another, and with our quest to make a substantial difference to the circumstances of our time. We carry these with us as life-long projects, and they can hardly be satisfied by cosmetic modifications, or shifts in lifestyle. Who we really are is much deeper than what we happen to look like at any given time. Put another way, I know that there is much more to me than meets the eye, or fills the ear. I have to live with myself. Rather, I have to love myself. But I must come to know who I am, and become fully engaged in a lifelong process of self-affirmation through that which is good within me, while seeking at the same time to accomplish a satisfactory measure of self-integration. For there should only be one me at a time. Self-recognition, then, lies deep at the heart of what it means to become engaged in a fresh search for God, in any and every age, or climate, or culture. As Christians, we are utterly con-

vinced that the God who is continually making and
remaking us knows us infinitely better than we know ourselves. This has nothing to do with the strange notions of
"the god within us," which are quite popular today. It is
only to restate the New Testament principle that to be
known of God, rather than to know God, is at one and the
same time to strive for a deeper knowledge of our own
selves, for self-recognition.

Second, we need a *sense of direction and purpose* in our
lives. It is an awful state of living when we have nothing to
live for, nothing to aim for, nothing to consider worth
attaining. The late Benjamin Mays has etched the unforgettable words on our memory that it is not a sin not to reach
the stars, but it is a sin to have no stars to reach. There are
stars and stars in the constellations that surround us and,
as Paul reminded us centuries ago, one star differs from
another star in glory. In that sense, then, there are some
stars that are not worth aiming for. We stand in constant
need of knowing how to distinguish the value of the stars in
our constellations of value and desire. For the Christian,
however, the sense of direction and purpose is not determined by the designs that we seek to create for ourselves.
Rather, it is determined by the saving work of God that is
already on the way through the meaning and message of
Jesus as the Christ of God. Jesus spoke of this work in terms
of the Realm of God, a topic to which we have repeatedly
returned throughout the course of this book. It is the bringing of the Realm of God into the affairs of our lives and cultures that should determine our sense of direction and purpose and should serve to meet this basic human need for a
sense of direction and purpose. Christians not only know
whose they are, but they also have a strong sense of why
they are here on God's earth, and where they are heading.

Third, since life itself is a constant battle, human beings
need *strength to fight.* The trouble is that we tend to inter-

pret the need to fight in terms of dominating one another. Paul reminded us centuries ago that the real wrestling, the central focus of the battle in the Christian life, is not really against each other but against the forces, the spiritual forces, that threaten our very existence. He wrote: "For our struggle is not against enemies of blood and flesh, but against the rulers, against the authorities, against the cosmic powers of this present darkness, against the spiritual forces of evil in the heavenly places" (Eph 6:12). As long as we are prepared to give a modern interpretation to what Paul expressed as the "cosmic powers," or the "spiritual forces in the heavenly places," and take our leave of the cosmology out of which Paul himself earnestly sought to escape, we are then free to recognize the spiritual forces of our own day against which we must constantly fight. These forces would certainly include emptiness, meaninglessness, meanness, depression, disillusionment, loss of values, and the threat of nothingness. The strong forces of alienation and *anomie* wreak havoc with our lives to such an extent that many prefer to give up the struggle and to find some form of refuge or escape through mind-altering drugs, or delusive lifestyles. We need to fight, and we need the strength to do so.

Fourth, the combination of the above-mentioned needs creates for us one focal point toward which, as human beings, we should always seek to strive. It is the point of *Shalom*—peace, wholeness, reconciliation of life, celebration of human existence, union with God. Deep within this need is the thought so powerfully expressed by Augustine of Hippo, the great African scholar and bishop, that God has made us for Godself, and that our hearts are restless until they find their rest in God. If God had made us to exist over against the rest of the created order, then perhaps this need for peace and wholeness might not have appeared to be so acute. But, because we are constantly in

existential dialogue with that by which we are surrounded, and from which we draw our physical nurture
and sense of well-being—that is to say, the world of
nature—we wrestle with the need to be at one with the
rest of creation, even if our baser instincts drive us to
believe that we would be better off by conquering it. This
has less to do with our ecological responsibility as such,
and much more to do with our spiritual, moral, and relational selves as bearers of the very image of God as our
Creator. This has everything to do with *personal integration,* the critical quest of becoming one with our very
selves. Human wholeness and personal integration are
inseparable factors in our vision of *shalom.* The human
need for *shalom,* then, is the need to come to terms with
that which God has made us to become.

These four basic human needs should serve to point us in
a certain direction when we begin to explore the meaning
of spirituality itself, and the possibility of a new spirituality
for the ministry to which God calls us at this critical junc-
ture of our human history. For there is clearly a need for the
healing of the human and structural brokenness in our culture. There is clearly a need for a fresh discovery of hope in
the face of ever darkening despair, brought on by the
unimaginable depths to which human depravity has sunk.
For example, we should take no pride in having to
acknowledge that the twentieth century has been the
bloodiest in all of human history. It is believed that more
persons have died in wars and human conflicts in this century than in all the previous centuries put together. In any
event, our capacity to destroy the inhabited earth more
than six hundred times over, because of our nuclear capa-
bilities, should fill no human heart with any sense of domination. "Abomination" comes more readily to mind. The
two greatest horrors of our present century have clearly
been the Jewish Holocaust in Europe, and the White

Afrikaaner apartheid scourge in South Africa. Future historians will undoubtedly treat these two epochs as signatures of this century, in spite of our tremendous accomplishments in such spheres as science, industry, technology and medicine. Given these overwhelming needs and historical realities, therefore, what kind of spirituality do we seek as the contextual basis for Christian witness and ministry for these times? Let us see what a preliminary discussion on contextual spirituality would look like.

Spirituality in Context

In his very helpful discussion on the inextricable connection between "spirituality" and "liberation," found in his book *Spirituality and Liberation: Overcoming the Great Fallacy,* Robert McAfee Brown has drawn our attention to some important insights relating to the context of spirituality. He makes use of William Stringfellow's catalog of the caricatures surrounding spirituality, which is worth quoting in full:

> "Spirituality" may indicate stoic attitudes, occult phenomena, the practice of so-called mind control, yoga discipline, escapist fantasies, interior journeys, an appreciation of Eastern religions, multifarious pietistic exercises, superstitious imaginations, intensive journals, dynamic muscle tension, assorted dietary regimens, meditation, jogging cults, monastic rigors, mortification of the flesh, wilderness sojourns, political resistance, contemplation, abstinence, hospitality, a vocation of poverty, nonviolence, silence, the efforts of prayer, obedience, generosity, exhibiting stigmata, entering solitude, or, I suppose, among these and many other things, squatting on top of a pillar.[81]

Brown goes on to add to these wide and varying caricatures of spirituality four "overlapping charges" against
it which are widely held. These are: "Spirituality is other-
worldly; spirituality is individualistic; spirituality is an
endeavor for the elite; "spirituality produces no impetus
to work for change."[82] With all of these charges, of course,
Brown would entirely disagree, and he proceeds to
demonstrate, mainly through the prism of Latin American
liberation theology and praxis, that spirituality and liberation are basically two sides of the same coin. In redefin-
ing "spirituality" therefore, Brown asserts that "spirituality when radically understood includes what is meant by
liberation,"[83] and further that "liberation when radically
understood includes what is meant by spirituality."[84]

Brown, of course, has been greatly influenced by the
writings of that great Latin American liberation theologian, Gustavo Gutierrez. For although he has become
famous for his extensive work and leadership in the area
of a theology of liberation, it must never be forgotten that
for Gutierrez, a spirituality of liberation has constantly
been at the center of his thoughts and writings. He has
always understood spirituality to mean the dominion of
the Spirit. He pays special attention to the need of living
before the Lord in solidarity with fellow human beings, for
it is through the leading of the Spirit that we are guided
to complete freedom, "the freedom from everything that
hinders us from fulfilling ourselves as human beings and
offspring of God and the freedom to love and to enter into
communion with God and with others. It will lead us
along the path of liberation because 'where the Spirit of
the Lord is, there is liberty'(2 Cor 3:17)."[85] Gutierrez links
Christian spirituality to the life of commitment to the
process of liberation, the centrality of conversion to our
neighbors and those who are oppressed, and the living
sense of gratuitousness. He says that we are filled with the

sense of "the knowledge that at the root of our personal and community existence lies the gift of the self-communication of God, the grace of God's friendship, which fills our life with gratitude. It allows us to see our encounters with others, our loves, everything that happens in our life as a gift."[86]

There is undoubtedly a very wide range of plausible answers to the question, "What is spirituality?" Clearly spirituality means different things to different people, and to different classes of people. A recent collection of responses to that question, published in the monthly journal *Episcopal Life* (February 1997), revealed an interesting variety of opinions. One woman wrote: "I have come to know that spirituality resided just beyond the welcome mat of my own home. It grew in my mother's cherishing smile, my dad's staunch support and in my husband's love and companionship." Another woman wrote: "Spirituality is living each day with God." Still another: "Spirituality to me is the feeling of being at one with my fellowman and my Redeemer. It's a feeling of knowing that I will never be alone again, no matter where I am, because the Lord has so filled my life that I can connect with others wherever I am. It is what I sometimes describe as a feeling of being at home in the world." One woman was very scientific in her description: "It is the life-giving dimension which humanizes our capacity to love, to care, to laugh, to cry, to soar, and to give glory. It is our own unique DNA which identifies us as God's own." One clergyman put it this way: "Spirituality is a response to God. It is seeking the vision of God and the restoration of our being."[87] The famous Anglican superior of the Society of Saint John the Evangelist, the Reverend Martin Smith, has recently spoken about his own "compassion for words," especially those that have been stretched too far. One such word, he said, is the word "spirituality." It stands in need of a companion. Smith suggests that "the word *spirituality* cries out for the companionship of other words. It would yield some of its burden back to *prophecy*."[88] Smith remains convinced that prophecy is "the authority of the future. Life is not governed by precedent but by the future."[89]

One of the more progressive writers on the subject of spirituality today is Professor Michael Downey, a Roman Catholic scholar, who is the founding North American editor of *Spirituality,* and also editor of the *New Dictionary of Catholic Spirituality.* He has offered us a very rich and signal discussion on the ranges of spirituality and the varieties of approaches to the subject in his recent book *Understanding Christian Spirituality.* He suggests that, in general terms, "spirituality" refers to "the deep desire of the human heart for personal integration in light of levels of reality not immediately apparent, as well as those experiences, events, and efforts which contribute to such integration."[90] He argues quite cogently that an authentic awareness of the sacred must involve much more than an individualized and privatistic approach. It must include a "clear sense of belonging to a community," as well as a "clear sense of critical social responsibility."[91] Downey rightly suggests that Christian spirituality "*is* the Christian life itself lived in and through the presence and power of the Holy Spirit; it concerns absolutely every dimension of life: mind and body, intimacy and sexuality, work and leisure, economic accountability and political responsibility, domestic life and civic duty, the rising costs of health care, and the plight of the poor and wounded both at home and abroad."[92] Downey's ideas open for us a wider range of review on the fundamental question about what we really mean by "spirituality."

In their historic document *What We Have Seen and Heard* (1984), to which we have already referred, the black Roman Catholic bishops had described black spirituality as having four main characteristics: "it is contemplative; it is holistic; it is joyful; it is communitarian." "Ours is a spiritual heritage," they said, "that always embraces the total human person." The bishops maintained that it was this special gift of the Holy Spirit to black people which provided them with a sense of God's presence and power, and "taught our ancestors that no one can run from him and no one need hide from him" (pp. 8–11).

The Roman Catholic Bishops' Committee on the Liturgy has expressed its endorsement of these characteristics in their document *Plenty Good Room*. For example, they suggest that "African American spirituality explodes in the joy of movement, song, rhythm, feeling, color, and sensation."[85] They also have suggested that the African "spirituals" provide an invaluable source of expression of the African American spirituality. These "spirituals" express some very crucial aspects of their lives: "their anguish in slavery, their trust in God's mighty arm, their belief in God's care, their identification with Jesus' suffering, a suffering like their own, their belief in the resurrection, their desire for freedom, their assurance of certain freedom, their need for constant conversion and prayer."[93] The Committee of Bishops also asserted that it was a spirituality "born of moments of the African American sense of 'conversion'."[94]

Father Joseph Brown, the Roman Catholic scholar, has also offered us some very helpful insights on African American spirituality. He establishes a very close connection between the Old Testament story of the wounding of Jacob and African American spirituality. He contends that "the wounding of Jacob and the bearing of his true and deeper name seem [sic] the special province mapped out by African American spirituality...."[95] This spirituality finds its uniqueness especially in the role of the angel. Brown explains it this way: "The plain where Jacob wrestles with his angel is truly the place 'where God strives.' It is America. The founding ancestors of the spirituality presented here were denied the tents, flocks, tribes, riches, and possessions of either Jacob or Esau. They were not denied an awareness that their inheritance, their prophesied birthright, had been stolen from them. Choosing to reinforce their place in the telling of the story, they created a mystic space where truth is timeless, in the sense of being forever in the present."[96] This deeper awareness is reinforced by a set of qualities inherent in the African American culture, expressed in song and ritual, as well as by the virtues of *generosity* and *hospitality*. These virtues, Brown says, are "frequently choked by 'American values' of individualism, selfishness, suspicion, and jealousy."[97]

I once raised the question of spirituality with my doctor of ministry seminar students at the Howard University School of Divinity. I was struck by the similarity of the responses they made, especially in view of the brief time they were given to do so. Some of their responses went like this:

> *Spirituality is a state of communication with God the Spirit.*
> *It is a relationship with God.*
> *It is the development of one's encounter with the Spirit of God.*
> *It is the submission of one's life to the Holy Spirit.*
> *It means dealing with the forces—values, virtues, ideals—which elevate us spiritually.*
> *Spirituality is life in the Spirit.*
> *It means dealing with the inner spirit and developing it.*
> *Spirituality means growing progressively in commitment and submission to the will of God.*

With such a varied sampling of responses to the meaning of spirituality, there can certainly be no question that we are brought face to face with the fact that no aspect of the life of the spirit takes place in a vacuum. Neither ritual, nor theology, nor spirituality, nor prayer is culture-free.

The ethical and moral constructs by which we seek to govern ourselves and guide the minds of those committed to our care are always conditioned by the context in which we find ourselves and them. Thomas Moore is therefore on the right track when he speaks of spirituality in its broadest sense as "an aspect of any attempt to approach or attend to the invisible factors in life and to transcend the personal, concrete, finite particulars of this world," and reminds us that "spirituality is not always specifically religious."[98] I would go further to say that it is not *often* specifically religious. There are real forces within our consciousness and our context which drive our way of thinking and acting, and which override any sense of the relationship with the divine—*often* at critical moments of our lives.

This is perhaps what Moore is getting at when he states: "In our spirituality, we reach for consciousness, awareness, and the highest values; in our soulfulness, we endure the most pleasurable and the most exhausting of human experiences and emotions. These two directions make up the fundamental pulse of human life, and to an extent, they have an attraction to each other."[99] He contends that whenever spirituality and soul are split apart, a narrow fundamentalism takes over. We need always to be focused on a spirituality which embraces the depths of our soul, as well as our persistent yearning for freedom from all forms of bondage which deny the fullness of our human dignity and destiny as children of the Most High God. While Moore arrives at his position from a background of religion and pastoral counseling and therapy in the North American context, it might be useful for us to look at another view of spirituality from the other side of the Atlantic in the work of Kenneth Leech, a British theologian and clergyman.

In his widely acclaimed work *Experiencing God: Theology as Spirituality,* Leech contends that the quest for spirituality through various methods, including drugs, since the 1960s, has been linked to the desire for ecstasy and salvation instantaneously. He refers to this as the spiritual undergrowth which has been part and parcel of an idolatrous society. Leech suggests that "idolatry is in essence a failure of vision, a diminished level of consciousness. Idols can be seen, touched, confined. Idolatry may take the form of packaged religion in which, for a fee, God-consciousness can be acquired."[100] Leech therefore called for "spiritual discrimination and discernment between the phoney and the authentic, between the false gods and the true God."[101]

After an extensive survey and wide-ranging discussion on the ways in which God has been experienced from Abraham onwards, and the several trends in modern theological exploration, Leech eventually offers what he calls a manifesto toward a renewed spirituality. This renewed spirituality, he says, should be concerned with recovering the vision of God in the modern world, rooted in the God experienced by the Jewish people, but finding its center in Jesus Christ and expressed through the faith of the apostolic church in the New Testament. It should be a spirituality "of the desert, of cloud and darkness, of water and fire," deeply rooted in the Incarnation, and celebrative of the "eucharistic life of sharing and equality in the world." This renewed spirituality should be one of pain, following the way of the cross, yet learning to see God as "the ground of all reality and of our own beings." It should take the experiences and just expectations of women seriously, in the light of the God of love and justice, as well as "to know and follow God in the pursuit of justice for all people." Leech concludes with these words: "In the struggles for a more human world, a renewed spirituality will come to discern the face of God, the holy and just One, and to share in the peace of God which passes all understanding."[102]

There is certainly a great difference between making prescriptions for what a basic form of spirituality should entail, and what it really means for persons in the existential situations and circumstances of their lives. To a very real extent, spirituality is both public and private, both personal and societal, biographical and metaphysical, historical and ideological, rooted in story and vibrant in theory, resourceful for reflection on the past, yet essential for any serious anticipation of the future, interpretive of experience, yet responsive to expectation. Perhaps a brief reflection on the testimonies of three very significant and historic personalities in this, the last quarter of the twentieth century, will give further expression to what we are getting at here. These three personalities are: President Jimmy Carter of the United States, and Archbishop Desmond Tutu and President Nelson Mandela of South Africa—all of Nobel Peace Prize stature. Although President Carter has not yet been granted this award, there is widespread global opinion that his frequent nomination to the Nobel Committee effectively places him in the league with the other two men who have already received it.

In his very moving book, *Living Faith,* President Jimmy Carter has invited us into his personal story about the meaning of faith for him as he has attempted to make the best use of his life, in the service of others and in loyal obedience to God. He states that the focus of his book is to "explore some of the ways my Christian faith has guided and sustained me, as well as the ways it has challenged and driven me to seek a closer relationship with God and my fellow human beings."[103] He speaks of his life as being varied and dramatic as president and professor, farmer and activist, parent and spouse, sailor and sibling. Throughout all of this life, he says, "my faith as a Christian has provided the necessary stability in my life. Come to think of it, stability is not exactly the right word, because to have faith in something is an inducement not to dormancy but to action. To me, *faith* is not just a noun but also a verb."[104]

As a national leader, he has constantly had to consider very carefully the relationship between his religious beliefs and his duties as an elected official. The many insights which he provides for us in this testimony demonstrate for us a very moving way in which the meaning of spirituality at the highest level of national decision-making, or at the very center of global political power (whichever aspect commands our greater attention), has its central place in the mind and heart of a person of faith. President Carter revealed that while in the White House he spent a large portion of his time trying to resolve difficult issues. The question which he posed to himself was this: "How could I join with others in feeding the hungry, clothing the naked, providing homes for the homeless, educating the illiterate, eliminating the stigma of poverty or racial discrimination, making peace and resolving differences between people, preventing crime, rehabilitating prisoners, and ensuring justice?"[105]

His valiant attempts to marry human rights concerns to the practice of United States foreign policy and foreign aid during his presidency has certainly marked out for him a special place in world history during the last quarter of this century. It would be difficult for us to assert that such a political option was not in keeping with the distinctive spirituality that has obviously guided his work during and after his sojourn in the White House.

The second person on whom we might reflect is Archbishop Desmond Tutu, the former Anglican Archbishop of Cape Town, South Africa. Throughout the long and bloody period of apartheid and racial oppression in

South Africa, many African leaders were dealt with by the governmental forces in several brutal and inhumane ways, to put it mildly. The African leaders of the churches were not immune from persecution, especially as the apartheid system was heavily reinforced by a theologically concocted scheme of racial separation, and aided by a belief in the divine election of Afrikaaners. While most of the African political leaders were silenced, or imprisoned, it fell to the religious leaders to be as courageously prophetic and persistently pastoral as was necessary for sustaining the hope of their people in the eventual overthrow of the demonic system of apartheid. Desmond Tutu, in his several appointed positions in the church, and through his active witness in the wider national and global community, preeminently embodied the meaning and measure of the resistance to all that apartheid stood for.

His messages, sermons, lectures, books, prayers, testimonies, crusades, and conferences all over the world served to bring before the world's eye the greatest blot on the conscience of modern civilization since the Jewish holocaust. Yet all of this was clearly rooted in a spirituality that often expressed itself in some very moving ways. Tutu once wrote: "God is smart, making us different so that we will get to know our need of one another. We are meant to complement one another in order to be truly human and to realize the fullness of our potential to be human. After all, we are created in the image of God who is a diversity of persons who exist in ineffable unity."[106] Tutu has been very consistent in his Christian anthropology, namely that the dominant theme of *imago dei,* the belief that all of us are created in the image and likeness of God, has far-reaching implications for the pursuit of justice and freedom, as well as for our obligations to each other. His operative spirituality has been centered around this all-embracing theme.

The harsh realities and grave indignities which he and his fellow Africans have encountered have indeed made the meaning of suffering an important element in the life of the Christian, as Tutu understands it. Frequently, he would draw attention to the extent of the sufferings of himself and his people; but it was never in the context of the inevitability of revenge. It was always in the context of hope seasoned with the meaning of Christian solidarity. For example, the following excerpt amply describes Tutu's spirituality: "If you are to be a Christlike leader then you must say with Paul: We preach Christ crucified and ourselves as your servants for Christ's sake. Suffering is not optional. It is of the essence of Christian discipleship and leadership."[107]

But suffering can also have another side, especially when those who were once the oppressed assume the upper hand. Tutu's sense of inevitable victory over the oppression would not permit him to be unaware of the continuing need to be a loud drum major for justice. Thus, in the same breath with which he speaks of the meaning of suffering discipleship, he also speaks of the need for vigilance: "We have all been greatly blessed by God in the privilege we have had to witness and minister against apartheid. And sometimes we have had our witness, all of us, authenticated by different kinds of suffering. We have tried to witness for justice and equity. We will still have to be around to be the voice of those who will be marginalized and voiceless in new dispensations in our countries, when we may have to speak critically against those whom we championed previously."[108]

The spirituality of suffering gives way to the spirituality of victory. In Tutu's thoughts, it is victory of light over darkness, life over death, truth over the lie, freedom over oppression, justice over injustice. Yet it is a victory of gentleness, kindness, goodness, compassion, sharing, peace, and reconciliation. He therefore urges his fellow citizens to commit themselves to discipline, peace, negotiation, and reconciliation.[109] This is the context in which we are to understand the establishment of the Truth and Reconciliation Commission in South Africa, headed by Tutu himself, which was to examine all the atrocities of the apartheid system and to grant amnesty for those who confessed their complicity.

Such a novel response to the aftermath of the South African holocaust is obviously in stark contrast to the response to the earlier holocaust in Germany, where Nazi war criminals have been rounded up globally for trial for the past fifty years or more. The spirituality of *reconciliation* and forgiveness demonstrated by the African experience constitutes in this century a striking alternative to the spirituality of *retribution* demonstrated by the European experience. The *justice of reconciliation* has in the course of our most recent history come into a creative and fertile encounter with the *justice of retribution,* and African spirituality has been at the fore of this dynamic global interface between one form of justice and another. The moral, historical, religious, and political implications of such an interface would make for a very penetrating and enlightening discussion. But that would take us too far afield from our present concerns at this time. Only time will tell what are the abiding lessons to be learned about the collective response to evil and injustice, as well as about the true meaning of a spirituality that is grounded either on the power of freedom, or else on the freedom of power.

The focus on *reconciliation* has always been a major factor in the public discourse and proclamation of the Christian message. There have been many different ways in which fractious groups have attempted to interpret its meaning. Most of these ways have often been cast in the mold of enlightened self-interest or the enhancement of one person's position over another's. Nevertheless, the inextricable connection between *reconciliation* and *justice* must not be obscured in any public search or struggle for genuine reconciliation. This point was made very strongly by the black Roman Catholic bishops in 1984 in their pastoral letter *What We Have Seen and Heard.* The bishops reminded us that "without justice, any meaningful reconciliation is impossible. Justice safeguards the rights and delineates the responsibility of all" (p. 7). In a very profound exposition on *reconciliation,* the Bishops affirmed: "Reconciliation can never mean unilateral elevation and another's subordination, unilateral giving and another's constant receiving, unilateral flexibility and another's resistance. True reconciliation arises only where there is mutually perceived equality. This is what is meant by justice" (p. 7).

When Archbishop Tutu was awarded the Nobel Peace Prize in 1984, Nelson Mandela was still the celebrated prisoner on Robben Island in South Africa. Mandela wrote a letter of congratulation to the Archbishop, but the prison authorities refused to send it. That prize meant much to Mandela, for Tutu had been the most prominent protagonist for African liberation from apartheid. Mandela recognized that that award was really for all the oppressed people of his country struggling for their freedom. But Mandela himself had been universally regarded as the preeminent human symbol of the liberation struggle, the "oracle of resistance," as one journalist put it, and the long years of his imprisonment constituted, for the racist regime in South Africa, their prolonged period of isolation from civilized global society and their increasing unpopularity throughout the world. How Mandela survived, and what his years of imprisonment meant for him and his people, is powerfully chronicled in his own words in his book, *Long*

Walk to Freedom, which he had secretly begun to write in 1974 during his imprisonment on Robben Island.

The spirituality which comes through from his autobiography is that of an African prince unswervingly committed to the total liberation of his people from their bondage in their own land; to the unconditional loyalty to his ancestors and his lineage for the protection of that which was rightfully theirs; to the establishment of a climate of justice which was based on the equality of all races before the law; and to the liberation of his oppressed people from poverty, undevelopment, and ignorance. For him, education was the most effective enemy of prejudice, and he recognized this both in his oppressors as well as in his fellow-oppressed. Was Mandela a Christian or a Communist? Representatives of a famous American newspaper sought to discover this when they once visited him in prison. In his own words, he reports thus: "I told them that I was a Christian and had always been a Christian. Even Christ, I said, when he was left with no alternative, used force to expel the moneylenders from the temple. He was not a man of violence, but had no choice but to use force against evil. I do not think I persuaded them."[110]

It is his undying love of freedom which best characterizes the spirituality and struggle of Mandela. His many years in prison actually prepared him for the art of leading a newly freed people into a new kind of freedom. When apartheid was eventually overthrown, therefore, and South African blacks finally assumed the commanding heights of their own sovereignty, there was already in place not simply a human icon, nor a living symbol, but an actual and active person, fully equipped mentally, morally, ideologically, and physically to take hold of the reins of power with graceful simplicity and universal approbation. What was it that so equipped him? Let Mandela speak for himself:

I never lost hope that this great transformation would occur. Not only because of the great heroes I have already cited, but because of the courage of the ordinary men and women of my country. I always knew that deep down in every human heart, there is mercy and generosity. No one is born hating another person because of the color of his skin, or his background, or his religion. People must learn to hate, and if they can learn to hate, they can be taught to love, for love comes more naturally to the human heart than its opposite. Even in the grimmest times in prison, when my comrades and I were pushed to our limits, I would see a glimmer of humanity in one of the guards, perhaps just for a second, but it was enough to reassure me and keep me going. Man's goodness is a flame that can be hidden but never extinguished.[111]

It would be very difficult for any careful analysis of the foregoing excerpt not to recognize in them the same theme of *imago dei* which Tutu has also affirmed in so many ways. The major contribution of Tutu and Mandela to our current understanding of spirituality is in the area of risking the meaning of forgiveness and reconciliation. They invite us to take seriously the possibility that love and goodness can still in the end overcome all the powers of evil and hatred, and to renounce any ideology of bitterness or revenge for the sake of getting even. No wonder then that Mandela appointed that Truth and Reconciliation Commission and designated Tutu as its leader, all for the sake of demonstrating their unswerving allegiance to the true meaning of freedom. Mandela said of himself that he was not just born with a hunger for freedom, he was born free, but that it was only after he realized that his freedom had been taken away from him that he began to hunger for it.

Nevertheless, in his emancipation from prison and in his assumption of power in his native land, he and his people had only achieved the freedom to be free, and the right not to be oppressed. "For," he wrote, "to be free is not merely to cast off one's chains, but to live in a way that respects and enhances the freedom of others. The true test of our devotion to freedom is just beginning."[112] His rationale for establishing the Truth Commission fits squarely into this spiritual and moral framework, for truth and freedom are inextricably bound together. Mandela affirmed the rightness of his cause in what the commission stood for with these words: "We can now deal with our past, establish the truth which has so long been denied us and lay the basis for genuine reconciliation. Only the truth can put the past to rest."[113]

There is something about the meaning of spirituality in the so-called Third World which is not only expressed so powerfully in the examples of Tutu and Mandela, but also in the reflections of other persons of color. These are the people who know what it means to suffer innocently, while at the same time bringing new life to others. Take for example the reflections of the Ghanaian theologian Elizabeth Amoah. For her, "the basis of a living spirituality today is preceded by a radical encounter with that which gives life and that which empowers men and women, young and old, rich and poor to be sensitive to, and to get involved with, life-giving activities."[114] She comments on the unjust and life-denying situations under which much of the world's poor are forced to live. Genuine spirituality, she says, requires getting in touch with life-giving activities, in touch with the spirit, or what she calls, "the PRESENCE." She also contends, however, that "an authentic and useful spirituality appreciates and respects the spiritualities of others. This makes it easier to team up with others for the struggles in life."[115]

This was the general trend of thought and reflection among Third World theologians who met in Nairobi, Kenya, in 1992 for the Assembly of the Ecumenical Association of Third World Theologians (EATWOT). In their final communiqué the participants issued the following reflection on spirituality:

> There is no room for romanticizing spirituality. It is a cry for life, a power to resist death and the agents of death. Spirituality is the name we give to that which provides us with strength to go on, for it is the assurance that God is in the struggle. Spirituality involves people's resistance to dehumanization and fulfills the quest for self-discovery, self-affirmation and self-inclusion, for in each of us in the whole human community is the urge to live and to live fully as human beings. It is the strength of the call to life that leads to various life-giving rituals of Native Americans and other indigenous peoples.[116]

The Caribbean region continues to be peopled by those who wrestle daily with the persistent problems of poverty, dependence, alienation, imitation and ecological instability. Nevertheless, our people in the region are generally driven by a relentless faith in the proposition that the Caribbean belongs to God, and that it is through faith in the God of Jesus, expressed in radically affirming and culturally regenerative ways, that their own spirituality will sustain their erstwhile fragile structures of existence. This is a spirituality that does not give up, even if at times it might appear to give in. Caribbean spirituality is indeed best understood as a spirituality of freedom, even if at times the echoes of slavery and fresh forms of bondage appear to be looming once more on their regional horizons. As I have written elsewhere, there is a constant reaching out in prayer and praise to the sovereign free God, and there is a relentless yearning for the empowering sense of a relational presence that is liberating, emancipatory, and affirming. Much more needs to be made of the daily spirituality that enables Caribbean people to cope with the pressures of life, and these spiritual forces must find their formal expressions in culturally relevant liturgies and hymnodies which characterize regional worship. Further, Caribbean theodicy has made faith stronger rather than weaker, and the church owes it to the broad spectrum of its membership to reflect more faithfully the tremendous depths of trust, hope, and courage which Caribbean spirituality generates.[117]

It is that constant cry for life, for new life, which must continually bring us into a radical encounter with what our deepest spirituality should convey. We must come to understand spirituality not merely in terms of that which goes on inside the individual, any individual, but also in terms of what goes on around the individual, between individuals, among groups of persons, and within institutions in our society. We must come to recognize that spirituality has less to do with what people feel inside of themselves, their hopes and fears, their dreams and prayers, their spirit and souls, and much more to do with all that makes people who they think they are at any given time. There is spirituality in the air we breathe, the sounds we hear, the sights we behold, the things we create, the movements we force, the institutions we sustain, the darkness we dispel, and yes, even the aura we generate. In a very real sense, our spirituality is us. Any determination to minister to persons in such circumstances will need to take into account the things which constitute this comprehensive climate, a climate which is neither sacred nor secular, neither straight nor crooked in its paths, neither weak nor strong in its force, neither full nor empty in its intensity. A new spirituality at the close of this twentieth century should therefore take serious account of a number of critical factors. It is therefore to a discussion of these factors we will now turn in our final chapter, as we bring these reflections to a close.

CHAPTER EIGHT

A NEW
SPIRITUALITY
FOR MINISTRY

As I BEGAN TO REFLECT ON THE PERVASIVE NATURE OF THE hungers that surround us at the close of the twentieth century, I reached back into the earlier volumes of this century for the writings of Howard Thurman. I was particularly anxious to review his book entitled *Deep Is the Hunger*. Thurman grouped his brief meditations into four categories—"Sense of History," "Sense of Self," "Sense of Presence," and "For the Quiet Time." The theme of hunger actually appears nowhere in any of his headings or subheadings. Nevertheless, the underlying quest for that which is needed to fill the void in human life is everywhere evident in what he shares with us in those pages. His reflections still reverberate in our souls even today, long after his passing from us.

Thurman does point us to a sense of restlessness, which seems to him to be inherent in the very structure of our human personality. He quotes someone as saying: "'Always roaming with a hungry heart,' this is man in his essential nature." This restlessness is otherwise referred to as "divine discontent", or the "homing instinct", or "the flight of the alone to the Alone." He tells of a modern poet who suggests that "God gave to man every gift but *rest* so that man would never be at ease, finally, except with God." "To the man who has found his rest in God," he says, "there comes the strength to reduce all the ill-at-ease-ness to manageable units of control, making for tranquility in the midst of change and upheaval."[118]

For Thurman, the "change and upheaval" to which he referred had to do with political revolution and social transformation in Russia, Europe, and Asia in the mid-1940s. For us today, we are in the midst of some major catastrophic and phenomenal episodes, some natural, some political, some criminal, and some religious. These episodes not only threaten our designs for tranquillity in the human spirit, but also beckon us to a fresh recognition of the depth of hunger and struggle to which so many of our contemporaries have taken themselves. Allow me to reflect on four episodes in the decade of the nineties which appear to me to have created more than a passing impact on the minds and memories of those in search of a new spirituality. These are: the Million Man March of October 1995, the volcanic eruption of Mount Soufriere on the Caribbean island of Montserrat, the mass suicide of the Heaven's Gate Cult during Holy Week 1997, and the deaths of Diana, Princess of Wales, and Mother Teresa in the summer of 1997. You may ask what these unrelated episodes have to do with spirituality. The answer lies somewhere in the strange meanderings of my own theological imagination, as well as in the fact that they are historic events of our times which have carried with them some metaphoric significance far beyond the immediate boundaries of the episodes themselves. Put another way, they constitute defining moments of our times.

Spiritually Defining Moments

One of the critical distinctions which Jesus of Nazareth made during his ministry was about the capacity of his followers, who were on the inside, to discern certain facets of life which those on the outside (*hoi exo*) could not. He said that his followers were given to know the mysteries of the Realm of God, and that those on the outside, even though they had ears, still could not hear, or had eyes, still could not see. The capacity to discern the spiritually defining aspects of ordinary episodes in our experience, then, in certain God-related ways, still remains for the Christian a very important dimension of our relationship with God through the Spirit. This is the basis on which I make bold to refer to those four recent episodes as spiritually defining moments of our times. They speak to us of a hunger, a dimension of suffering, and a relentless struggle, all of which seem to me to be integrally related to the meaning of Christian spirituality for ministry today. Let us look briefly at each of those moments in turn.

In October of 1995 the city of Washington, D.C. witnessed an event of historic proportions, reminiscent of the great March on Washington in the summer of 1963 which was led by the late Martin Luther King Jr. It was called the *Million Man March,* and it was essentially led by another prominent African American leader, Louis Farrakan. The March was called by Farrakan and his colleagues to bring black men together from around the country to reaffirm their commitment to the highest ideals of self-determination and self-sufficiency, to take responsibility for their own behavior, and to assume the commanding heights of their own liberation. It was summoned as a mass demonstration of commitment, rather than as a mass demonstration of protest. The common enemy was dubbed to be more within them than outside of them. The hunger for justice, the struggle for greater freedom and progress, as well as the struggle against the systemic sufferings of blacks, were understood to be the major points of focus.

Great controversy surrounded the head count of those attending the March. Estimates varied from as low as 400,000 to as high as over one million. But the numbers really did not matter. What mattered the most was the historic spectacle of such a mass demonstration of black men meeting each other in serious assembly and reaffirming their commitment to some high ideals, all based on the nobler instincts of human development and resolve. Such ideals were given mass expression and endorsement when Farrakan led the assembly in a solemn pledge. They pledged to: love each other as brothers; to work toward their own self-improvement; to build their own businesses; to promote non-violence; to respect women, who were the mothers of their children and the producers of their future; to renounce child abuse in any form; to refrain from using obscene epithets, especially relating to females; to avoid the use of drugs which abused the human body; and to support the black-owned media.

The significance of this defining moment surely lies in the fact that an attempt at mass spirituality was given historic meaning and relevance as the answer to a confluence of problems and issues affecting the plight of black men in America today. Here was an attempt to bring together men from around the country—black men, proud of their blackness and purposeful in their vision of a new set of possibilities for their own future. They came together to find new resolve and inspiration, not in identifying the traditional enemy, but in acknowledging the source of the pain, the common pain, and the possible means to some self-regulating and collective amelioration. Even if the American cancer of racism was at the root of all the pain and struggle, it was not being held up here as the primary focus of the struggle.

The Million Man March provided for the African American community a whole new way of speaking about the hunger, sufferings and struggles of black people in this country, and it did so through the demonstration of black solidarity, black pride, black spirituality, and black re-orientation. In short, it provided a new watershed in the unfolding saga of the Black Story, and created a new way of generating the seeds of a living memory, which is always so critical in the forward development of a people in struggle for their freedom. Future historians may be cynical enough to label it an event of mass euphoria, especially in light of their inability to link any significant follow-up action to the event itself. Only time will tell. But for those who participated in it, or witnessed it, there can certainly be no doubt that it provided, at least for the lingering moment, a pervasive sense of spiritual and moral empowerment, the likes of which no other political or social event in modern times had been able to produce for black men in this country.

The second episode has to do with the eruption of the volcano on Mount Soufriere on the Caribbean island of Montserrat. Montserrat happens to be my favorite Caribbean island, although I was born on the island of Antigua, just a stone's throw away. It has been called the "Emerald Isle" for many reasons, chief among them being the character and social quality of its native people. In my considerable experience among them, I have found that Montserratans are by nature among the strongest, hardiest, most resilient, independent, generous, unpretentious, loyal, self-reliant, and religious people in the Commonwealth Caribbean. It was my privilege to serve my first appointment as a parish priest (rector) of St. Peter's parish in that country, with three very vibrant and challenging congregations—Saints Peter, James and John—situated over mountainous terrain in the north of the island. This is where the remaining inhabitants of the devastated country have now huddled for safety.

What happened on Montserrat? The earliest European history records that European settlers arrived on that tiny island in 1632. It has to be assumed however that the island enjoyed a rich native history with Caribs and Arawaks inhabiting it long before the white men arrived. The volcano that had been dormant for over four centuries suddenly erupted in July of 1995. For two years afterward there were major eruptions, with massive clouds of ash, huge rocks, major bursts of steam, and devastating pyroclastic flows, all of which have rendered a large portion of the island no longer habitable. The capital city, Plymouth, was destroyed, and several people lost their lives. As a colony of Great Britain, Montserrat has received a lamentably small amount of aid and support from the United Kingdom, including providing only meager incentives for the Montserratans to resettle in other Caribbean islands, or even in England. Several Montserratan dogs have been allowed entry into the United States territories, while many persons have been refused. Nevertheless, a few thousand Montserratans decided to remain on their island home, come what may. Why would anybody wish to remain under such menacing conditions, with all the pain, suffering, loss, and struggle already experienced?

The answer lies somewhere in the deeply embedded spirit of a hardy people who are accustomed to the realities of nature, and whose courageous response to the harshness of the environment mark them as a special people of God's created order. My own encounter with Montserratans since the onslaught of the disaster has not brought me in touch with any expressions of self-pity, total despair, or anger at God. Rather, I have been struck by their pervasive determination to deal with this disaster in the light of a God who still loves them, and who maintains contact with them. One of my former parishioners put it this way: "God is trying to tell us something, Father, and we must listen." Another Montserratan said: "We don't know when the volcano will do something. The geologists do the best they can, but they don't know either. Only God is in control. We can only pray that when the next event comes, there is no danger to it. We still have to thank God that we have food and shelter and friends."[119] One American visitor to the island commented that faith is the islanders' bedrock. Most villages, no matter how small, have at least one church, and nearly everyone attends services dressed in Sunday best. Hymns ring across the hills from the front porches at sunset, an outpouring of devotion that helps people accept the upheaval. "'At first it really gets on your nerves, but then you put God first and everything smoothes out,' said a nursery school teacher."[120]

What does it really mean to put God first in the face of impending pyroclastic flows from a menacing volcanic mountain? How can the God of the mountain, so powerfully encountered in the history of the Jews and the story of Jesus, become the God of devastating ash and consuming fire, while remaining the God of love and the controller of nature? What does it mean to wait on a God who seems unwilling to stem the tide of volcanic calamity? The Montserratans are able to pose these questions with firsthand suffering and threatening experience. And yet, somehow, they are determined to hold on to a spirituality that neither curses God nor erodes their faith. Montserratan spirituality today is a defining witness to the meaning of faith as the common assurance of things not seen. Hunger, suffering, loss, and natural disaster have somehow provided for them a new understanding of what it means to trust in the unseen God of their salvation, in the face of very little empirical justification.

The third defining moment has to do with the shocking events of Holy Week 1997 here in the United States when, with the rest of the world, I was horrified by the news of the mass suicide of the members of the Heaven's Gate cult. Thirty-nine members of the group took their own lives in their desire to move on to a higher level of existence. This anticipated movement to a higher level was to have been achieved by joining a spaceship that would follow in the wake of the comet Hale-Bopp, then visible from earth.

Many have waxed eloquent about the whys and wherefores of this sad and awful tragedy of our time, drawing their own conclusions about the meaning of modernity and the dangers of modern science. Others have sought for fresh meaning about the quality of life in our modern era, and the tremendous sense of loss, loneliness, and despair which has often driven our contemporaries to make the unimaginable possible. *Washington Post* columnist E. J. Dionne Jr., for example, suggested that "a small proportion of human beings lose touch, are drawn to peculiar doctrines and, their personalities weakened by group attachment, slide into mass lunacy." For him, "the rationality we associate with the modern world is far from triumphant because modernity has created its own discontents." In a case such as this, he sees it this way: "The most advanced forms of modernity join forces with darker impulses that go back to the caves."[121]

Also, in *The Washington Post*, Vladimir Lehovich, a former United States diplomat, in a very profound reflection on the Heaven's Gate crisis, offered the following description of the movement:

> It professed a pseudoscientific view of another life in space. It suppressed normal instincts of sociability

and sexuality. It urged men to undergo castration. It required abandonment of possessions, family, friends and sometimes children. It fed on disoriented, dejected people on the fringes of society in whom it could produce quick conversion. It viewed the human body as a container and way-station between different incarnations of an inner essence. It said that the body can be physically transported to another world. It called for unquestioning allegiance to the group's directions. It viewed death as a welcome release to a higher existence; and it engaged in mass suicide. None of this is new.[122]

Lehovich went on to explain that new religions usually seek "society's weary, alienated and marginal." "Is quick conversion possible?" he asks, and answers: "Of course: The fishermen of Galilee on the spot heeded Christ's command to rise up and follow him. The greater the need and the pain, the stronger the attraction of an inclusive message." He predicts that as the end of the second millennium approaches, "we will see more new movements all over the world."[123] Modern-day Christians must never forget that the origins of the religion of Jesus of Nazareth filled many of his contemporaries with a great deal of cynicism, resentment, resistance, and mockery, especially with regard to the claims which his followers made about him after his death.

While it is historically true that Christianity started out as a "cult," with martyrdom and sacrifice among its chief social characteristics, it has never led its adherents to the internal human disaster, the likes of which we witnessed during Holy Week 1997. The Heaven's Gate disaster, therefore, to my mind, is yet another metaphor of the culture and times in which we live, and an authentic sign of the deep quest for meaning and maturity which, in so many millions of lives, continues to remain unfilled. The hunger is real, the hunger is deep, the hunger is ours.

The fourth defining episode has to do with the deaths of two very prominent world figures within a week of each other: Diana, Princess of Wales, who died on August 31, 1997, and Mother Teresa of Calcutta, who died on September 6, 1997. The women obviously functioned in different worlds, but they were very closely related in many ways, one being their very strong admiration of, and mutual respect and support of, each other. The photograph of Diana leaning over to bid farewell to Mother Teresa on a New York sidewalk in June 1997 will undoubtedly become a priceless symbol of the human face of power mixed with the deepest heart of compassion.

Both women achieved a remarkable degree of global notoriety and approval for their relentless and sacrificial efforts on the behalf of the poor, marginalized, dispossessed, and powerless members of the human family. Diana had dedicated herself to the cause of helping the homeless, the people with AIDS, and the victims of landmines. One writer said: "As the princess who would be Queen, Diana could turn the world's passion for her into compassion for others, whether they were the homeless, AIDS patients or casualties of land mines....She declared, 'Being permanently in the public eye gives me a special responsibility—to use the impact of photographs to get a message across, to make the world aware of an important cause, to stand up for certain values.'"[124] In one of the most remarkable twists of British and world history, the death of this lady had certainly demonstrated that, although she had lost her royal status, her fully human stature had remained intact.

This was obviously in the mind of her brother as he delivered the eulogy at her funeral in Westminster Abbey in London. Earl Spencer said, in part:

Diana was the very essence of compassion, of duty, of style, of beauty. All over the world she was a symbol of selfless humanity, a standard-bearer for the rights of the truly downtrodden, a very British girl who transcended nationality, someone with a natural nobility who was classless, who proved in the last year that she needed no royal title to continue to generate her particular brand of magic. Today is our chance to say thank you for the way you brightened our lives, even though God granted you but half a life....Without your God-given sensitivity we would be immersed in greater ignorance at the anguish of AIDS and HIV sufferers, the plight of the homeless, the isolation of lepers, the random destruction of land mines. Diana explained to me once that it was her innermost feelings of suffering that made it possible for her to connect with her constituency of the rejected....Diana remained throughout a very insecure person at heart, almost childlike in her desire to do good for others so she could release herself from deep feelings of unworthiness of which her eating disorders were merely a symptom.[125]

Diana's brother clearly understood her very well, and championed her memory in a most profound and unforgettable way. Others who presumed to know her also wrote of her as a living icon of selflessness and compassion, brought about by her own personal experience of suffering. For example, one article offered these telling words: "The lonely youngest daughter of divorced parents, she translated her own pain not into bitterness and withdrawal but into a genuine desire to comfort the suffering of others—people afflicted with AIDS and leprosy and breast cancer, the mutilated victims of land mines. She could have done far worse with her fortune and acquired fame."[126] Diana herself was often quoted as saying that the major disease in the world was that people were unloved. She therefore tried to use her considerable powers to redress that grave imbalance in the human family, wanting eventually to earn as her final epitaph the words: "A great hope crushed in its infancy." Her great hope was to relieve the world's suffering as best she could.

While Diana tried her best to use her considerable fame in the interests of the destitute, Mother Teresa of Calcutta spent most of her life in sacrificial service of the poorest of the poor in India, and other parts of the world. It has been well said that she remained a "sign of contradiction" to the world in her life, as well as in her death, for her "humility was burdened by celebrity. She raised millions for her work but lived simply, befriending the rich and famous to aid the poor and anonymous. She was a woman of power in a church run by men. Although a missionary of Christ, she insisted that God wanted Hindus to be good Hindus, Muslims good Muslims."[127] Mother Teresa had distinguished herself long before she was awarded the Nobel Peace Prize, because of her uncommon passion for the plight of the dying. She committed herself and the order she founded to ensuring that the poor of Calcutta and elsewhere could at least have a beautiful death for, as she said, she saw the face of Christ in each face of the dying. Suffering and death, for her, far from being the final statement of the meaning of human life, opened new ways of understanding the richness of the gift of life.

Mother Teresa therefore challenged the global church to live out, in the most concrete and practical ways, the central message of a gospel which claimed that God was unconditionally on the side of the poor and the oppressed. She managed to make suffering redemptive, not only for those who suffered, but for those who could bring themselves to understand in the deepest spiritual sense what it meant to worship and believe in a God who suffers with them. The sufferings of the poor were therefore redemptive not only for them, but for all who stood in solidarity with them. Father Andrew Greeley has rightly said of her that "the world knows that Mother Teresa is a saint and hails her as such. She represents the Christian faith at its finest and the Catholic heritage at its best. She was a light shining on the mountain, a light that death cannot extinguish." He also affirms: "If she is not a saint, then I don't know who could be."[128]

What is it then about the deaths of these two women, in such a close proximity of time, that has created a radically new defining moment for our times as far as spirituality is concerned? The answer lies in the fact that their deaths triggered a universal spirit of solidarity with the causes which they had championed, causes that revolved around the reality of human suffering in its many and varied forms. It was the poor and despised who made them universally famous and provided for the rest of us a challenging moment to touch our deepest souls, as sharers in one great human family whose Creator and Sustainer is God. Their deaths brought us all together for at least a shining moment of reaffirmation of the primacy of love and compassion, and the commonality of suffering and hope juxtaposed in each human breast.

Their manner of death was radically different—the one shocking, tragic, and unexpected, and the other peaceful, predictable, and climactic. Roger Rosenblatt has said that "the two women were united by an impulse toward charity, and charity is a tricky way to live....If love is based on the mystery of the person, then it becomes a glad concession to God's authority. Judgment of others is impertinent. One sensed that feeling in Mother Teresa—and in Princess Di as well—that the effort to help and sympathize superseded any wish to assess, and this was probably the ground on which they met in the South Bronx. A capacity for unjudging sympathy was certainly what the public admired in them."[129] It was therefore a most fitting tribute to the legacy of Diana, that although, unlike Mother Teresa, she was not awarded the Nobel Peace Prize, the latest cause with which she was prominently associated, the banning of land mines, was so honored in the award of the Prize for 1997.

These four defining moments can serve to draw our attention to some aspects of human life and livelihood that lie deep in the heart of those who yearn to be spiritually renewed. These aspects are elucidated by the realities of suffering and pain, hunger and emptiness, alienation and poverty of spirit, struggle and aimlessness. They confront the very canons and icons of power and success, of triumph and superiority, and beckon us to look again at ourselves in the light of what we see, hear, feel, and experience all around us in this global village.

They speak to us of people yearning and working for radical change and relief in their lives, and for radical breaks with the present, in order that some new divinely inspired reality might emerge in the clearer light of a brand new day. They offer us clues about what is often wrong with us, even if there is no volcano to run from, no cult to run to, no march to excite us, nor tragic death to frighten us. They speak to the deep hungers of our time, and to the yearning for the new power of the Spirit. How then does the search for a new spirituality for Christian ministry help us in our quest? It all depends on the nature of the ministry we seek, and the meaning of the power to which we aspire. Our concluding sections will focus our reflections on two critical issues concerning a new spirituality for Christian ministry.

The Ministry We Seek

Throughout the course of this book we have had occasion to reflect on the meaning of Christian ministry from a variety of perspectives. We have looked at the context of crisis in which we are constantly called to minister to God's people in God's world. We have examined the meaning of servanthood and friendship as two modes of understanding the Christian imperatives for ministry. The frontiers for new ministry, and the challenges of servant-leadership, both within the church and beyond, have also come into focus as we have surveyed what it means to follow Jesus as the Way. We have also spent some time exploring what is involved in practicing the art of the presence of God—a God who comes, rather than a God who calls from afar. All of this, when put together in a pattern of theological search for a more illuminating way of interpreting our sense of vocation as Christians, brings us face to face with the stark realization that we can accomplish nothing new without a strong sense of divinely inspired direction. In short, we stand in need of a new spirituality if we are to face the crises and hungers of our world today.

Our study of spirituality in the preceding chapter has undoubtedly left us with the notion that spirituality means different things to different people, and that it offers new thrusts in a variety of social contexts and cultural circumstances. The question then must be asked: is there any common ground? Can we speak of a common spirituality which touches adequately on the basic things which make us Christians, followers of the same Christ, members of the same global community of faith, inheritors of the same gospel of salvation, and agents for change in the same world, in the light of the coming Realm of God?

It seems to me that we can indeed do so, but only if we are prepared to take our cue from the one in whom we find our common reason for becoming whom we are called to become. We are called to be children of God, servants of the Servant, and sharers in the Community of the Spirit. We take our cue from our understanding of Jesus, not only as the Way *to* God, but also as the Way *from* God. The ministry we seek, therefore, is that which is rooted and grounded in the Way of Jesus of Nazareth, made known to us in the living and apostolic faith of the church, and held constantly before our notice by the message of the gospel proclamation. The ministry we seek is that which strives to be in faithful obedience to the One who simply urged: *Follow Me.* The ministry we seek is that which strives to embody in concrete, historical, and transforming ways, the message of salvation and wholeness which is offered to us through the life, death, resurrection, and indwelling of the Christ of God. The ministry we seek is none other than that lived out extension of the Incarnation, the fact of God the Creator becoming God the Inhabiter; the Ultimate Reality becoming known chiefly as the Intimate Reality; the Unknown God becoming the Very Present Help in Trouble.

Two focal points in the gospel tradition provide us with a major thrust for what we are saying here. One is the summary description of the ministry of Jesus of Nazareth given to us in Matthew's Gospel. The other is the injunction issued to Simon, as the leader of the new apostolic band, sometime during their Easter experience.

Jesus is described as the Great Teacher, Preacher, and Healer. "Then Jesus went about all the cities and villages, teaching in their synagogues, and proclaiming the good news of the kingdom, and curing every disease and every sickness" (Mt 9:35). It is important to point out here that the generally promulgated concepts of the triple office of

Jesus—Prophet, Priest, King—are not supported in the gospel tradition. Even if a prophetic consciousness is explicit in the gospel, the overriding theme of the suffering servant of Deutero-Isaiah becoming fulfilled in Jesus of Nazareth casts a heavy veil over any notion of Jesus as the King, or Jesus as the Priest. For Matthew, the ministry of Jesus is a matter of function for the sake of God's saving will, not a matter of office or status for the sake of the people's hierarchy of power. It is not the acquisition of wealth and power, but his confrontation with evil, ignorance, and disease that consumes the ministry of Jesus in the gospel. His life and example of total, unconditional, and filial obedience to God is demonstrated principally in this triple ministry of teaching-preaching-healing.

Whatever we might say about the origins of the Johannine traditions in the New Testament, whether in respect to authorship, dating, apostolic authority, or anything else, it must be clearly understood that we have in the Fourth Gospel a very important aspect of the living faith of the early church. It is a lively faith in Jesus as the Christ of God, which obviously takes into account a familiarity with the Synoptic tradition of Mark, Matthew, and Luke, and which provides for us windows into the life of the apostolic community which would otherwise have remained hidden from our knowledge. One of the windows which the Gospel of John opens for us is a clear and unmistakable understanding of what was to be the main focus of the ministry of those who were to be leaders of the followers of Jesus. The followers of Jesus are his sheep, for he is the Good Shepherd.

Those who would lead the followers of Jesus are required to care for the sheep, fully recognizing that they belong only to Jesus. This is the light in which we are to understand the injunction to Simon Peter in John 21:15–17: *Feed my lambs....Tend my sheep....Feed my sheep.* The command to feed and tend the sheep presupposes the constancy of need on the part of the followers of Jesus. There is a sense of vulnerability and dependence, a sense of need for solidarity and guidance, a sense of yearning for sustenance and safety. All this is to be done on the behalf of, in the name of, and for the sake of, the One who has already given his life for the sheep. Sacrificial suffering has already brought a new sense of solidarity between Shepherd and sheep, a solidarity which needs to be strengthened and sustained by teaching, preaching, healing, and tending, as well as by feeding. This is the totality of the ministry we seek. Or it might be more correct to say that this is the totality of the ministry that is seeking for us. What does this require of us? Five pivotal virtues come readily to mind.

First we must be driven by an *intelligent faith;* that is to say, a faith that is serviced and sustained, strengthened and renewed, challenged and refreshed by deepest treasures of our divinely empowered intellect. The "children of light" must themselves be the bearers of the Light.

Second, we must be unconditionally and hermetically sealed by a *personal commitment to Jesus Christ* as the Lord, the only Lord. The attractiveness of mammonism, and the subtle appeals of enlightened self-interest, must always be renounced as incompatible elements of a Christ-centered life.

Third, we must be constantly summoned by the higher call to *moral courage,* not in the service of that which is convenient or expedient, but in faithful obedience to that which is right, just, and true, in the light of our obedient response to the demands of the gospel.

Fourth, we must seek to develop and maintain *healthy relationships* that promote the edification of the redeemed community, rather than the extension of the masses of the blissfully alienated. To support the lifestyle of that which blissfully alienates us and others from God, and from the noblest levels of our calling as Christians, is at one and the same time to further obscure that image of God in us which Jesus Christ came to restore at Calvary. We crucify the Son of God afresh.

Fifth, we are to be consumed by an outpouring of *inexhaustible compassion*. The supreme symbol of the cross in our Christian tradition stands unparalleled in its capacity to keep us active in our struggle to re-live, to re-present, to re-create, to re-invigorate, and to re-proclaim the compassion of Christ to all those whom he came to set free. Compassion is not merely an option for the Christian, it is a must.

It is with these five virtues, then, granted to us through the constant agency of divine grace and healing, that we make bold to place ourselves at the point of contradiction and paradox in a world we still really do not understand. Nevertheless, this is the only world in which it has pleased God to place us. This is the world, the only world, in which we are called to minister to others at the very point at which we are ourselves being ministered to by God, in some strange and unpredictable ways. For finally, it is only those who know what it is to be ministered to by God who can truly come to understand what it means to minister to others for the sake of God.

We minister always as earthen vessels to earthen vessels, all sustained by powers unknown and yet real, all surrounded by cracks in our nature yet wholesome enough to bear the Spirit of Christ, the Expiator, who covers over the cracks in our vessels and make them new. We see the sufferings of our times, the pains and struggles of our age, and the pervasive helplessness of our spirits as cracks, wide cracks, in our lives. Yet, it is that new spirituality that emerges from a fresh realization of the cracks in our earthen vessels which, oddly enough, bring us new surges of faith, new vistas of hope, and new reasons to love. They make it possible again for us to renounce the modern temptations to be in the *service of power,* and to recommit ourselves to be spiritually, emotionally, and morally consumed by the *power of service.*

Serving with Power

Any new spirituality for Christian ministry, therefore, must fully take into account all the contextual, historical, cultural, and religious forces that drive our sense of worth and well-being. Many of these forces have been hinted at in all that we have been discussing so far. As long as we are prepared to understand the life and function of Christian ministry in terms of faithful, loyal, and obedient service in the light of God's mission of total and unconditional salvation, then the primary focus for the new spirituality will be on the question of "who," and not on the question of "what." The latter flourishes in sacred posturing, flashy rhetoric, and bankable clichés, while the former thrives on the gradual realization of what it means to be a full person. "Personhood" and "personality" are two different things, and very often they tend to be at war with each other. For while we cannot escape from our personhood, we can always make convenient and political adjustments to our personality. What then are the elements of this new spirituality?

I believe we should interpret our spirituality in narrative terms—as the ongoing story of our life, our *curriculum vitae.* Spirituality incorporates the memory of our past, the hidden realities of our present condition, and the inevitable consequences that lie in the unfolding circumstances of our future. For better or for worse, our spirituality consists in the coming together of our personal experiences, our choices of expression, and the urgings of our deepest expectations, and provides us with our continuing life story. For the Christian, this is best understood in terms of its theological, moral, and socio-political dimensions, and these dimensions suggest a number of crucial implications for the pursuit of Christian witness in the modern world, and the practice of Christian ministry for the sake of Christ. Let us briefly outline these dimensions and their implications.

The theological dimension consists of the meaning of *Christus Victor.* What does it mean to profess the faith that Christ has won the victory? Victory over what? Victory for whom? How does the Resurrection faith become the art of Christian living?

The moral dimension consists of the centrality of *Christlike Virtue.* That is to say, the strength by which we live must somehow reflect the meaning of Paul's: "I live, yet not I, but Christ lives in me." Christian spirituality does not cater for two lives at the same time.

The socio-political dimension consists of the primacy of *Christian Values* as the basis for Christian conduct, Christian culture, and Christian service. This is where our witness to the in-breaking of the Realm of God comes into a daily struggle with the forces of evil and the Gospel of Common Sense. Christian values is almost always antithetical to that which is expedient, or practical, or convenient. Why? Because it takes its orders from the cross, and the cross is the supreme symbol of confrontation, contradiction, and con-summation—the highest meeting of pain with love.

These three dimensions then, *Christus Victor,* Christlike Virtue, Christian Values, serve to provide the basic infra-structure, the Disk Operating System (DOS), the Windows of a new spirituality. They provide the minister, the servant of Christ, with the readiness to encounter, and respond to, the spiritual, moral, social, and personal challenges in the lives of the people of God. There are eight such challenges.

(1) *The Efficacy of Prayer and Praise.* We live in an age of much experimentation and questioning concerning the spiritual dimensions of health problems, addictions, and alternative forms of medicine. The effects of the intense uses of mental energy on the states of the physical body are being heralded as a great discovery in the delivery of health care. None of this, however, should directly, or indirectly, affect our basic life of faith in the God who not only calls us into being, but by whose grace we are sustained, whether in life or death. The efficacy of our prayer or praise to God is not determined by our physical or material well-being. It is determined solely by our complete, unconditional, and total sense of dependence on God. Our post modern forms of spirituality must never seek to generate new ways of measuring results, or of calculating effects. The efficacy of divine prayer and praise lies wholly in the fact itself, and is never conditioned by any outcomes. Persons of faith are never fearful of God's mysterious ways.

(2) *The Morphology of Pain.* As fellow participants in the human condition, we all must suffer pain. Indeed, it is perhaps true to say that we are who we are because of our capacity to suffer. The central message of the Christian Gospel is that through our faith in Jesus Christ, and in our sharing vicariously his life of perfect sacrifice, we understand the meaning of redemptive suffering. But all suffering is not redemptive. Much of it remains mysterious, unjustified, destructive, and diminishing. Pain takes on innumerable forms, as it strikes with innumerable dimensions. It is the challenge of the servant of God to be constantly aware of and responsive to this amorphous world of pain. The servant of God must be ever mindful of the fact that the face of pain might appear in the most attrac-

tive disguises, or that the voice of pain might be heard through the most melodious sounds. All that glitters is not golden. In other words, more people hurt in more ways than we can ever know, or fully understand.

(3) *The Boundaries of Pleasure.* As beings who are susceptible to the world of pain and suffering, we are also sharers in the world of pleasure. For most people life is not all dull all of the time. There is much which pleases the heart, mind, body and will. Indeed, it is perhaps true to say that most of our time, talents, and resources, are dedicated toward the achievement and enjoyment of that which is pleasurable. The global entertainment and communications industry is perhaps the best yardstick for such a measurement. Yet, pleasure challenges our basic rights and obligations to our human family. We are seduced by its powerful lures and we rationalize our own indulgence, very often at the expense of others' rights and freedoms, or of the moral fabric of wholesome society, or even of the responsible use of our creative intellects and human imagination. The new spirituality for ministry must recognize and affirm that there are boundaries to the pursuit of pleasure, and that these are to be guarded and reaffirmed by a faithful commitment to the full worth and dignity of every human soul, created in the image and likeness of God.

(4) *The Sacramental Nature of Human Passion.* Just as we have spoken of pain and pleasure as inherent dimensions of the human condition, we need also to speak of human passion. Human beings are persons with feeling—emotional beings whose basic structure enables them to respond to the experiences within themselves, and beyond themselves, with varying levels of intensity. But there is much more to these feelings than we can ever comprehend. There is something sacramental about them. That is, we are endowed with such by some divine intention. They help

to accentuate our sense of the being of God in our world. They lift us out of ourselves to a higher order of reality. Human passion then is a means to a greater, higher end, rather than just the measure of who we are. It is an earthly fact with a heavenly meaning. We have never clearly understood why Jesus wept for Lazarus, his friend, but he wept. The challenges for the servant of God in this regard, then, are simply enormous. At the very least, we are challenged to be non-judgmental of that which we least understand, since we are *all* passionate beings. Further, we are challenged to bear witness to the sacramentality of each other's passions in a way that will enhance the saving work of Christ's liberation of human nature, as well as the reality of God's creative and life-giving love.

(5) *The Transparency of Power.* The four challenges which we have outlined deal directly with the human condition, and with ourselves as persons. Yet, we are also beings in community and our spirituality is directly affected by the contours of social context, as well as by the means at our disposal for participating in the social process. This is why the principal theme of the gospel relates to the Realm of God—that rule of God in the hearts of humankind, individually and collectively. This has to do with power. It has to do with who exercises it, and how it is exercised. It has to do with the ways in which power serves the development and dignity of each human being, or else retards that development. The exchanges between Jesus of Nazareth and Pontius Pilate the Governor are instructive here. Yet, it is the paradox of the cross of Christ which at one and the same time displays the superiority of power (to take innocent life), as well as the transparency of power, (there is nothing else to take). The new spirituality for Christian ministry must help God's people to discern the transparency of power, in whatever form it comes, so that the levels of intimidation and threats of nothingness

can be confronted by a divinely inspired sense of eventual elimination. Power almost inevitably self-destructs. It pays to wait on the God who is the ultimate source of all power.

(6) *The Call to Penitence.* Just as we are often diminished by the abuse of power, so we are also assaulted by the abuse of freedom. This is what we mean by SIN. Sin is the abuse of our God-given freedom. There are structures of power which are designed to enhance and strengthen the better ordering of society. But there are also structures of power which inhibit such ordering. Similarly, there are sinful structures which are reinforced by the abuse of human freedom, and which consequently generate social relations and habits of living which are inherently evil. Laws and institutions, modes of social exchange and entertainment, patterns of behavior and classes of association, are all susceptible to this reality. Sin abounds both individually and corporately. The spirituality involved in the "Call to Penitence," then, requires of us that constant sense of *metanoia. Metanoia,* or repentance, is a radical renunciation of the social and political structures, the personal and collective habits of living, which deny the emergence of God's saving and reconciling grace toward human wholeness. Human wholeness is not possible without an utter and unconditional renunciation of the alienating structures of sin in our culture. This is the meaning of the Call to Penitence. No human being, nor human agency, can claim any exemption or state of innocence.

(7) *Solidarity on the Edges of the Periphery.* We are constantly reminded in the gospel that the Son of Man came to be identified with the poor, the lost, the lonely, the enslaved and the destitute. The authentic image of Jesus in the gospel provides us with the "man-for-others" symbol. He is the symbol of sacrifice, sharing, solidarity, suffering and salvation. Indeed, Jesus of Nazareth speaks of such people as his brothers and sisters. They are referred to as

"the least of these." From this image we make bold to proclaim that the God whom we worship, and to whom we
seek to bear witness, is unreservedly and unconditionally
on the side of the poor and the oppressed. These are
people who exist not just on the edges of life, but on the
edges of the edges of life. They are, as it were, *the least of
the least.* Our new spirituality for Christian ministry must
in every way seek to repudiate any attempt to establish
floorboards in our structures of ministry, or fixed boundaries in our reach of care and concern. The image of a
church and its ministry that exempts itself from reaching
down or reaching out because of extreme circumstances,
or exceptional conditions of pain and suffering, is antithetical to the gospel of Jesus Christ. There is no one for
whom Jesus did not die, or to whom the love and care of
God cannot be extended. It is through our encounter with
those on the edges of our world that we can truly come to
a fuller and fiercer understanding of what is involved in
taking up the cross and following the Crucified One as a
daily exercise in ministry.

(8) *The Certainty of Divine Promise.* One of the greatest
temptations for the servant of God today is to be cynical
and despondent. Cynicism is a modern and up-to-date
cultural pastime, which is fed and nurtured (?) by our
sense of enlightenment and mastery of knowledge, by an
increased proclivity toward a benign self-conceit, and a
heightened awareness of the fragility in our personal relationships and social structures. Our level of trust in the
value and worth of human effort is thus diminished, and
our capacity to trust that which we do not fully understand is heavily assaulted. The life of faith thus becomes
more burdensome, and our sense of impotence to stem the
rising tide of evil and its devastating effects diminishes
our sense of hope. It is against this background that the
servant of God must reaffirm the certainty of faith in the

One who has promised to be with us all the time. No spirituality for ministry will be worth very much unless there is that underlying and sustaining sense of the presence of God, the promise of God, and the power of God, all working together with the spirits of those whose hope is built on the certainty of God's future. In so far as the minister is able to bear concrete witness to the belief that God's future is being brought into this uncertain present, it is to that same extent that the totality of ministry, feeble though it may be, will be able to provide God's faithful people with sufficient courage to trust in the trustworthiness of God. That trustworthiness consists of nothing less than God's faithfulness to God's promises. For the One who creates is the One who recreates. The One who has promised is the One who has always delivered. As the old folks would say, God may not deliver when we expect, but God always delivers on time! God's delivery and our deliverance are inextricably bound together in our life of faith.

All of these challenges, therefore—*Prayer and Praise, Pain, Pleasure, Passion, Power, Penitence, Peripheral Existence, Divine Promise*—raise some very broad and critical issues for the character of Christian ministry for today and tomorrow. It seems to me that we will not be able to break much new ground unless we are prepared to deal with them openly, honestly, prayerfully, intelligently and courageously. The new spirituality demands that we take new risks for Christ in our postmodern world. For whether it is the question of pain or pleasure, or the issue of power or passion, the "children of this world" continue to offer to the "children of light" tempting and intriguing ways of coping and surviving, but not for overcoming. Yet the "children of light" offer little or no resistance, nor do they seem to make much room for any higher or better alternatives. The new wine from above can hardly find suitable wineskins here below.

Serving with Power

Christian ministry remains in crisis, therefore, apparently more readily attracted to the service of power, than to being transformed by the power of service.

●

We can hardly do better than to conclude our entire discussion in this book with some words from the late Henri Nouwen:

> The great paradox of ministry, therefore, is that we minister above all with our weakness, a weakness that invites us to receive from those to whom we go. The more in touch we are with our own need for healing and salvation, the more open we are to receive in gratitude what others have to offer us....The true skill of ministry is to help fearful and often oppressed men and women become aware of their own gifts, by receiving them in gratitude. In that sense, ministry becomes the skill of active dependency: willing to be dependent on what others have to give but often do not realize they have....True servants depend on those whom they serve. They are called to live lives in which others guide them, often to places they would rather not go.[130]

Notes

1. *The Washington Post,* September 5, 1995, p. A5.
2. *The Washington Post,* August 29, 1995, p. A3.
3. Ibid.
4. "Episcopal News Service," August 1995.
5. See "Book Review," *The New York Times,* March 8, 1992, p. 24.
6. Francis Schüssler Fiorenza, *Foundational Theology* (New York: Crossroad, 1984), p. 212.
7. *The Washington Post,* February 2, 1991, p. G1.
8. Robert N. Bellah, et. al. eds., *The Good Society* (New York: Alfred A. Knopf, 1991), p. 104.
9. Stanley Hauerwas, *After Christendom?* (Nashville: Abingdon, 1991), p. 107.
10. *But We See Jesus* (New York: Episcopal Commission For Black Ministries, 1990), p. 22.
11. *What We Have Seen and Heard,* A Pastoral Letter on Evangelization from the Black Bishops of the United States (Cincinnati: St. Anthony Messenger Press, 1984), p. 23.
12. Ibid.
13. *Plenty Good Room: The Spirit and Truth of African American Catholic Worship* (Secretariat for the Liturgy and Secretariat for Black Catholics, National Conference of Catholic Bishops, Washington, DC, 1991), p. 37.
14. Joseph A. Brown, S.J., *To Stand on the Rock* (New York: Orbis, 1998), p. 186.
15. Ibid.

16. Edward Schillebeeckx, *Ministry* (New York: Crossroad, 1981), p. 70.

17. Frank Allan, "'Cheating' At Church," in Barbara Brown Taylor ed., *Ministry and Mission* (Atlanta: Post Horn, 1985), p. 74.

18. Edward Schillebeeckx, *Ministry,* pp. 31–32.

19. See Tilden H. Edwards, ed., *Living With Apocalypse* (New York: Harper & Row, 1984), pp. 19–20.

20. Jurgen Moltmann, *The Way of Jesus Christ* (San Francisco: Harper & Row, 1990) p. xiv.

21. Howard Thurman, *Meditations of the Heart* (Richmond, Indiana: Friends, 1976), p. 49.

22. Howard Thurman, *Meditations,* p. 175.

23. Eugene H. Peterson, "Twenty-Three years...Persistently," *Weavings,* Vol. IX, No. 4, July/August 1994, p. 26.

24. Michael Downey, "Making A Way," *Weavings,* Vol. IX, No. 4, p. 9.

25. Rosabeth Moss Kanter, *Commitment and Community: Communes and Utopias In Sociological Perspective* (Cambridge: Harvard University Press, 1972).

26. Michael Downey, op. cit., p. 15.

27. See Conrad Cherry, ed., *Horace Bushnell : Sermons* (Paulist Press: New York, 1985), p. 80.

28. Ibid., p. 81.

29. Ibid., p. 93.

30. R. E. C. Browne, "Courage," in John MacQuarrie, ed., *Dictionary of Christian Ethics* (Philadelphia: Westminster, 1967), p. 76.

31. Nelson Mandela, *Long Walk To Freedom* (Boston: Little, Brown & Company, 1994), p. 542.

32. Richard Stoll Armstrong, *The Pastor As Evangelist* (Louisville: Westminster Press, 1984), p. 68.

33. See *The New York Times,* Sunday, March 8, 1992, p. 19.

34. Ibid.

35. Jean-Bertrand Aristide, *In the Parish of the Poor* (New York: Orbis: 1990), p. 90.

36. See Herb Miller, *The Vital Congregation* (Nashville: Abingdon, 1991), pp. 123–33.

37. See *The New York Times*, Sunday, March 1, 1992, p. E15.

38. Ibid.

39. Ted Peters, *The Cosmic Self* (San Francisco: Harper & Row, 1991), p.ix.

40. Ibid.

41. See Earl E. Shelp and Ronald H. Sunderland, eds., *The Pastor As Servant* (New York: Pilgrim Press, 1986), p. 41.

42. Ibid., p. 42.

43. Jurgen Moltmann, *The Way of Jesus Christ* (San Francisco: Harper & Row, 1990), pp. 42–43.

44. *But We See Jesus* (New York: Episcopal Commission for Black Ministries, 1990), P. 17.

45. Vincent Harding, *Hope And History* (New York: Orbis, 1990), p. 181.

46. Robert N. Bellah, et. al., eds., *The Good Society* (New York: Knopf, 1991), p. 49.

47. Ibid., p. 218.

48. Paul Tillich, *Theology of Peace* (Louisville: Westminster/John Knox, 1990), p. 34.

49. Wolfhart Pannenberg, *Theology and the Kingdom of God* (Philadelphia: Westminster, 1977), p. 76.

50. Anton Houtepen, *People of God* (New York: Orbis, 1984), p. 134.

51. Bruce Chilton and J. I. H. McDonald, *Jesus and the Ethics of the Kingdom* (Grand Rapids: Eerdmans, 1987), p. 79.

52. William Willimon, *What's Right with the Church* (San Francisco: Harper & Row, 1985), p. 58.

53. See *Le Sottisier*, xxxii. Quoted in *The Penguin Dictionary of Quotations* (Middlesex, UK: Penguin Books, 1964), p. 407.

54. Quotation from Douglas Steere by Dean Freiday. See "Friends/Quakers," *Dictionary of the Ecumenical Movement* (Grand Rapids: Eerdmans, 1991), p. 428.

55. Stanley Hauerwas, *After Christendom?* (Nashville: Abingdon, 1991), p. 94.

56. Walter Kasper, *Theology and Church* (New York: Crossroad, 1989), p. 91.

57. Isabel Anders, *The Faces of Friendship* (Cambridge: Cowley, 1992), p. 10.

58. Ibid., p. 14.

59. C. S. Lewis, *The Four Loves* (London: Fontana, 1964), p. 83.

60. Robert Neville, *A Theology Primer* (Albany: SUNY, 1991), p. 60.

61. Anders, op. cit., pp. 133–34.

62. See Barbara Brown Taylor, ed., *Ministry and Mission* (Atlanta: Post Horn Press, 1985), p. 146.

63. Robert N. Bellah, et. al., eds., *The Good Society* (New York: Alfred A. Knopf, 1991), p. 218.

64. See Earl E. Shelp and Ronald H. Sunderland, eds., *The Pastor As Servant* (New York: Pilgrim Press, 1986), p. 37.

65. Ibid., p. 42.

66. Ibid., p. 76.

67. Ibid., p. 79.

68 Richard Bondi, *Leading God's People: Ethics for the Practice of Ministry* (Nashville: Abingdon Press, 1989), p. 61.

69. Ibid., p. 62.

70. Robert N. Bellah, et. al., op. cit., p. 286.

71. Peter Hodgson, *Winds of the Spirit: A Constructive Christian Theology* (Louisville: Westminster/John Knox, 1994), p. 60.

72. Jurgen Moltmann, *The Spirit of Life: A Universal Affirmation* (Minneapolis: Fortress Press, 1992), pp. 238-9.

73. Walter Kasper, *Theology and Church* (New York: Crossroad, 1989), p. 146.

74. Ibid., p. 147.

75. Peter Hodgson, op. cit., p. 299.

76. Jurgen Moltmann, op. cit., p. 258.

77. See *Newsweek*, February 10, 1997, p. 65.

78. See *The Washington Post Magazine*, February 9, 1997, p. 21.

79. Ibid., p. 25.

80. James Melvin Washington, ed., *Conversations with God* (New York: HarperCollins, 1994), p. 266.

81. Robert McAfee Brown, *Spirituality and Liberation* (Louisville: Westminster Press, 1988), p. 36.

82. Ibid., p. 116.

83. Ibid., p. 121.

84. James B. Nickoloff, ed., *Gustavo Gutierrez: Essential Writings* (Minneapolis: Fortress, 1996), p. 287.

85. Ibid., p. 289.

86. See *Episcopal Life*, February 1997, p. 18.

87. See *The Living Church*, August 10, 1997, p. 12.

88. Ibid.

89. Michael Downey, *Understanding Christian Spirituality* (New York: Paulist Press, 1997), p. 26.

90. Ibid., p. 25.

91. Ibid., p. 45.

92. *Plenty Good Room*, p. 49.

93. Ibid., pp. 35–36.

94. Ibid., p. 48.

95. Joseph A. Brown, S.J., *To Stand on the Rock* (Maryknoll: Orbis, 1998), p. 82.

96. Ibid., pp. 84–85.

97. Ibid., p. 185.

98. Thomas Moore, *Care Of The Soul* (New York: Harper-Collins, 1994), p. 232.

99. Ibid., p. 231.

100. Kenneth Leech, *Experiencing God: Theology As Spirituality* (New York: Harper & Row, 1985), pp. 20–21.

101. Ibid., p. 23.

102. Ibid., pp. 421–22.

103. Jimmy Carter, *Living Faith* (New York: Times Books, 1996), p. 5.

104. Ibid., p. 4.

105. Ibid., p. 109.

106. Desmond Tutu, ed., *An African Prayer Book* (New York: Doubleday, 1995), pp. xiv–xv.

107. Desmond Tutu and John Allen, eds., *The Rainbow People of God* (New York: Doubleday, 1994), p. 237.

108. Ibid., p. 238.

109. Ibid., p. 254.

110. Nelson Mandela, *Long Walk To Freedom* (Boston: Little, Brown & Company, 1994), pp. 453–54.

111. Ibid., p. 542.

112. Ibid., p. 544.

113. See *The Washington Post,* February 21, 1997, p.A21.

114. See K.C. Abraham and Bernadette Mbuy-Beya, eds., *Spirituality of the Third World* (Maryknoll: Orbis, 1994), p. 51.

115. Ibid., p. 53.

116. Ibid., p. 198.

117. Kortright Davis, *Emancipation Still Comin'* (Maryknoll: Orbis Books, 1990), p. 141.

118. Howard Thurman, *Deep Is the Hunger* (New York: Harper & Brothers, 1951), p. 5.

119. See *National Geographic,* Vol. 192, No. 1, July 1997, p. 70.

120. Ibid.

121. See *The Washington Post,* Saturday, March 29, 1997, A17.

122. See *The Washington Post,* Saturday, April 12, 1997, A23.

123. Ibid.

124. See *Time,* September 8, 1997, p.35.

125. See *Newsweek,* September 15, 1997, pp. 25–26.

126. See *Time,* September 15, 1997, p. 40.

127. See *Newsweek,* September 22, 1997, p. 25.

128. Ibid,. p. 35.

129. See *Time,* September 15, 1997, p. 116.

130. Henri J. M. Nouwen, *Gracias!* (San Francisco: Harper & Row, 1983), p. 19.